DATE DUE

FAMILY THERAPY MODELS

Michael S. Kolevzon, D.S.W. and **Robert G. Green, Ph.D.** are Associate Professors in the School of Social Work at Virginia Commonwealth University. Dr. Kolevzon teaches research and family therapy courses in the M.S.W. program and coordinates the core curriculum in the Ph.D. program, where he has also taught research and program evaluation. Dr. Green coordinates the research content area of the M.S.W. program and the school's computer facility. He teaches courses in human behavior, family dynamics, and research methods.

Both authors regularly present clinically- as well as empirically-based papers at the meetings of the National Council on Family Relations and the American Association for Marriage and Family Therapy. They have published individually and collaboratively in such interdisciplinary journals as *Family Process, Journal of Marital and Family Therapy, American Journal of Family Therapy,* and *Journal of Divorce.* Dr. Kolevzon and Dr. Green have been, respectively, Research Project Coordinator and Research Associate of a major three-year-outcome project on family therapy intervention models. In addition, Dr. Kolevzon served as a special consultant and grant reviewer for the National Institute on Drug Abuse.

The current research interests of both authors converge on the dynamics of interpersonal relationships and on the research methodologies used to understand them. Dr. Kolevzon's research focuses on the impact of father/daughter relationships on adult women's personal and professional life choices, and Dr. Green has a special interest in the marital relationship and the dimensions of optimal family functioning.

FAMILY THERAPY MODELS
CONVERGENCE AND DIVERGENCE

Michael S. Kolevzon, D.S.W.
Robert G. Green, Ph.D.

SPRINGER PUBLISHING COMPANY
New York

Springer Publishing Company, Inc.

536 Broadway

New York, New York 10012

85 86 87 88 89 / 10 9 8 7 6 5 4 3 2 1

Library of Congress Cataloging in Publication Data

Kolevzon, Michael S.
    Family therapy models.

    Includes bibliographies and index.
    1. Family psychotherapy. I. Green, Robert G. II. Title.
RC488.5.K65   1985   616.89'156   85-7936
ISBN 0-8261-4450-0

Printed in the United States of America

To Ken: Indeed, there have been many times when the seemingly limitless nature of my own horizons captured me with a sense of frustration that goals once attained failed to become self-sustaining. At what point would I allow myself to rest, enjoying that which I had grasped and not solely the challenge of that which lay beyond my reach? And then, as I pondered my own parents' lives of limitless horizons, I realized that their sense of contentment ultimately was born not from the goals that they grasped but from the gifts that they gave, to their family and to their friends. And so, at last, what becomes important and self-sustaining for me is captured in my son, Kenneth. He is a radiant and beautiful gem, nurtured by his parents, to be sure, but so finely polished by divine nature. As a gift to the next generations, so too is he a gift to me, his father. He allows me to be at peace with him, with my own parents, and with myself.

This book is in tribute to my family which preceded me,
and in appreciation of my family which follows.

m.s.k.

For Frances Drewry Green, my wife, in commemoration of our twentieth wedding anniversary, with remembrance of the swinging bridge on which we first met, and for accompanying me across many subsequent bridges and helping me to cross those I had to negotiate alone.

r.g.g.

Contents

Preface

This book represents the crossing of the career paths of two friends and colleagues interested in the study of family dynamics and the process of the therapeutic encounter. The path of one evolved from the study of human behavior, and moved toward an appreciation of clinical practice, under the sobering yet inspiring guidance of the scientific enterprise. The other's path moved from scientific inquiry to the study of human behavior through the enterprise of clinical practice. While the messages are many, we trust that this book will represent a strong reaffirmation of the undeniable necessity for the clinical practice and research enterprises to be joined as partners in their search for an understanding of the human condition and for finding ways by which those involved in serving people may become more competent and confident helping professionals.

Acknowledgments

The five-year undertaking that this book represents, beginning in the winter of 1978 with the initial instrument pretesting and subsequent mailings, inevitably generated tremendous personal and professional indebtedness to many individuals who helped to make such a project possible. While we could not possibly mention everyone by name, we are deeply appreciative of the assistance, support, and patience that all of our friends and colleagues afforded to us during the course of this project.

We do want to express a special indebtedness, however, to Elaine Rothenberg, whose support for the scholarly activities of her faculty while she was Dean of the School of Social Work is evidenced by the Scholarly Leave program that she initiated and which, in turn, made possible the completion of this book. So too does our present dean, Grace Harris, deserve our sincere appreciation. In her first year as dean she has already displayed a vibrant determination to strengthen our school's commitment to faculty scholarship, and her assistance in securing the support services required for finishing this book has been unwavering. We also wish to acknowledge the encouragement and cooperation of Dr. Murray Bowen, Jay Haley, and Virginia Satir, whose assistance made our study possible and whose monumental contributions to the field of family therapy have provided direction for both this book and the interdisciplinary profession it has attempted to study.

While this book represents the culmination of an exciting and rewarding project and, we hope, the beginning of new projects yet to be fully formed, we must also express our special appreciation to Drs. Ruth Goldberg, Ted Goldberg, Jacob Hurwitz, Charles Lebeaux, and Leon Lucas (at Wayne State University); to Drs. Joseph Axelrod and Bernice Madison (at San Francisco State University); to Dr. Kermit Wiltse (at the University of California, Berkeley); to Dr. David Israel (of Richmond); to Dr. Lionel Lane and Professor Mort Schumann (at

Virginia Commonwealth University); to Dr. Ross Speck (of Philadelphia); to Professor Louis Carter (at the University of Pennsylvania); and to Dr. Michael Sporakowski (at Virginia Polytechnic Institute and State University), who, at varying points in our professional careers, provided us with the inspiration to risk and grow as well as with the models by which to guide this growth. They are all truly special people, and we will always be grateful for their friendship.

FAMILY THERAPY MODELS

1

The Emergence, Development, and Growth of Family Therapy

The practice of psychotherapy emerged as a recognized professional activity almost 100 years ago. During this period at least a half dozen different professions have laid claim to legitimacy and proficiency with regard to helping individuals with the problems of living. Concomitant with their growth, these helping professions have developed and proliferated diverse points of view about how humans behave and how, in times of need, they may be helped. Indeed, recent estimates suggest that at present there are between 130 (Parloff, 1979) and 150 (Abt & Stuart, 1982) different psychotherapeutic approaches distributed within and across the mental health professions. Most attempts to clarify and classify these schools suggest that they all are branches of or have historical antecedents in three organizing perspectives about human behavior: the psychodynamic, the behavioral, and the humanistic (Goldfried, 1982).

The majority of the practitioners oriented to these perspectives, in accordance with the basic premises of the points of view they represent, attempt to accomplish their treatment goals by attending to the expressed, observed, or inferred problems of individual patients or clients. While the psychodynamic, the behavioral, and the humanistic perspectives each partially explain human behavior with regard to the client's social context, the basic unit of behavioral explanation, and consequently of therapeutic intervention, across these points of view is the individual. As such the world view of these diverse perspectives about human nature can be considered nominalistic (Warriner, 1956). This prevailing point of view in American psychiatry suggests that the groups into which humans organize themselves are less "real" than are the individuals themselves. Rather, the group for all practical purposes is viewed as a contextual or background element of the individual. Consequently, the dynamic properties of groups are less important to the explanation of human behavior than are the dynamic qualities of individuals. Since individuals are viewed as the only or primary reality, the unit of explanation, and consequently of intervention, is the behavior of individuals—singularly or collectively.

Over the past 30 years, however, a rapidly increasing number of mental health professionals have challenged or rejected the nominalistic paradigm in favor of its antithesis, realism. This philosophical position holds that the group is as real as the individual and that it may be understood with reference to its own dynamic properties and processes, not by individual psychologies.

In this book we will be concerned with the clinical practice of one such group of mental health professionals—the family therapists—who, in a relatively short period of time, have challenged traditional and nominalistic assumptions about human behavior by focusing their therapeutic activities on the family group rather than the individual patient or family member. While they find meaning in the individual problems or symptoms exhibited by their patients, these manifestations are viewed as consequential or covariate aspects of family relationships. Consequently the patient or the client for family therapists is the family group rather than the individual, and their intervention targets improvement in overall family functioning or in specific intrafamily relationship systems.

While most family therapists tend to agree that the purpose of family therapy is the improvement of the functioning of the family group as a whole, the cumulative literature of the field suggests that, like their nominalistic therapeutic predecessors, considerable variation has emerged among family therapists in regard to their explanations for why families function as they do and how they may be helped. On the one hand this variation or diversification within the field might be viewed as a realistic and indeed perhaps desirable expression of the expanded bodies of knowledge resulting from attempts to explore, understand, verify, and communicate ideas concerning how to intervene to help families cope with the problems of living. Indeed, several theorists of the professionalization process suggest that such segmentation within a profession or discipline is a vital element that both characterizes and determines the nature of its growth (Bucher & Strauss, 1961; Carlton, 1977; Vollmer & Mills, 1966).

On the other hand, while this diversification may allow for more flexibility in the process of knowledge expansion, thereby perhaps permitting us to avoid the historical pitfalls of psychodynamic theory building (Schaefer, 1976), it also might have negative consequences. Indeed, a number of family therapy practitioners and researchers have warned of the dangers inherent in the process of proliferation of the many "family therapies." They have cautioned that the major proponents of family therapy have been attending to the "merchandizing" of their own techniques rather than focusing on the commonality of thinking within the field and on the impediments to the development of a unified theory of family therapy (Gurman & Kniskern, 1981; Liddle, 1982; Olson, Russell, & Sprenkle, 1980; Simon, 1980). A major dilemma confronting the evolving profession of family therapy, therefore, is one of maintaining efforts to expand and verify its knowledge and skill bases while at the same time identifying and preserving the bridges of common beliefs and techniques that unify the profession and guide the growth and development of its members.

In order to address this dilemma, however, the family therapy movement, as it increasingly has been named, must have a clearer inventory of both the shared and divergent systems of therapeutic belief and action that characterize its members. While the past 30 years have spawned a number of systematic conceptual attempts to classify the field, there has been a paucity of empirical efforts to profile areas of both convergence and divergence in regard to the belief and action systems of varied theoretical orientations in the family therapy field. This book seeks to fill this need with one such beginning attempt.

Consequently, in the present chapter we will provide an overview of the emergence, development, and growth of the family therapy movement. In Chapter 2 we will attempt to organize the diversity that has accompanied this growth by reviewing attempts to typologize the variations in theoretical orientation that have developed over the past 30 years. In Chapters 3, 4, and 5, we will call upon two data sets from practicing family therapists to serve as an empirically based "reality test" for the conceptualizations of the diversity within the family therapy profession discussed in the first two chapters.

A Different Paradigm

In *The Structure of Scientific Revolutions,* Thomas Kuhn (1970) describes the manner in which dominating thought systems or scientific paradigms appear to change over extended periods of time. He observes that changes or paradigm shifts do not result as a function of sequential or cumulative knowledge-building processes. Rather, they tend to occur in response to new discoveries about phenomena, often viewed as radical breakthroughs. These breakthroughs tend to follow periods of time in which particular belief systems have become institutionalized within particular scientific communities; these belief systems consequently provide a rather pervasive consensus on the manner in which phenomena are explained and predicted. Because of the comfort with this consensus, however, ideas that are not isometric with and indeed may be antagonistic to the prevailing paradigm often are rejected or ignored, in spite of their potential validity. Kuhn refers to these institutionalized states of knowledge equilibrium as periods of "normality."

Such a state of "normality" characterized the mental health professions in the late 1940s and early 1950s. The dominant psychiatric paradigm was clearly the nominalistic psychoanalytic perspective, and its attendant focus was on the treatment of individuals. By the end of World War II, psychiatry had become an attractive and increasingly legitimate specialization within the medical profession; consequently the enrollments in medical schools and psychiatric residency programs were flourishing and increasingly populated by students and teachers who previously might have been engaging in their research and teaching in the more isolated psychoanalytic institutes (Guerin, 1976).

There was no precedent during this period for conceptualizing the family as the unit of treatment. Although Flugel's seminal volume on the family (*The Psycho-analytic Study of the Family,* 1921) addressed the study and treatment of psychopathology within each family member, the psychoanalytic tradition prescribed individual treatment of individual family members for individual psychopathologies. Similarly, in the nonmedical helping professions, the idea of treating the functioning of a family group was a notion whose time had not yet come. Although social work as a profession had its origins in the provision of services to families (Rich, 1956), and although pioneering social workers such as Zilpha Smith (1890) and Mary Richmond (1917) wrote convincingly about their contacts with poor and needy families, the profession itself was impacted significantly by the psychiatric profession in the 1920s, and the treatment methods employed by social workers were somewhat wedded to those utilized by psychiatry. In a similar manner, psychology as a discipline and the emerging interdisciplinary profession of marriage and family counseling took the lead from the individualistic perspective that dominated psychiatry.

The Emergence of Family Therapy

As historians of the family therapy movement consistently have suggested, the discovery of family therapy cannot be attributed to a singular founding parent (Broderick & Schrader, 1981; Guerin, 1976; Hoffman, 1981; Kaslow, 1982). Rather, it grew from the research and experimentation of a number of mental health professionals in the late 1940s and early 1950s. Like the products of other scientific revolutions, however, it emerged from the frustration and dissatisfaction with currently sanctioned ideas and methods. Most of the ideas that subsequently provided the foundation for family therapy practice did so under the rubric of research (Bowen, 1975). Indeed, it was behavior that was observed "in its natural habitat" (Hoffman, 1981) that led to the simultaneous discovery of family therapy on both the western and eastern seaboards of the United States.

The Western Seaboard

In the early 1950s, Gregory Bateson, an anthropologist on the faculty of Stanford University, received a grant to further his study of human communication at the Veterans Administration Hospital in Palo Alto, California. Bateson had long been interested in the social systems of animal life and had become intrigued with Whitehead and Russell's philosophical notion of a hierarchy of logical types (Whitehead & Russell, 1910). Essentially this formulation highlights the paradox and confusion that results when different logical types of communication clash with each other. For example, when the sender of a message makes the statement "I'm lying" to an intended receiver, the receiver is faced with the dilemma of deciding whether the *content* of that message is true or whether the *context* of the message ("I expect you to believe what I say") is true. Paradoxically, the message is true only if it is false and false only if it is true.

Noting that the language of schizophrenic children often contained an abundance of these paradoxical statements, Bateson sought to explore their manifestation and function in human life. Consequently he brought together a diverse and talented team of researchers. The team included a communications expert (Jay Haley), a philosopher and chemical engineer (John Weakland), and later a psychiatrist (Donald Jackson).

As a result of their research and collaboration, in 1956 this group published a paper that was to become one of the most controversial in the history of American psychiatry. In "Toward a Theory of Schizophrenia" (Bateson, Jackson, Haley, & Weakland, 1956) they advanced the notion that schizophrenia was the resultant condition of a particular type of family communication. They argued, in what has become known as the double-bind theory, that schizophrenia was produced in a family context in which a command or injunction at one communicative level was repeatedly negated or contradicted at another. As such the paper suggested that schizophrenia, which previously had been understood as a thought disorder by psychodynamic psychologies, may indeed represent the paradox and confusion engendered by individuals who spend their developmental years in families where confused and illogical communication is the norm.

Over the years the double-bind theory has been tested empirically with mixed results (Berger, 1965; Olson, 1971, 1972; Weakland & Fry, 1962), modified (Bateson, 1972; Berger, 1978), expanded in scope to explain neurotic, psychosomatic, and behavioral disorders (Sluzki & Veron, 1971), and utilized as theoretical grounding for a variety of therapeutic intervention techniques (Andolfi, 1974; Watzlawick, Weakland, & Fisch, 1974; Weeks & L'Abate, 1982). However, the primary contribution of the double-bind formulation, beyond benchmarking the Kuhnian paradigm shift, has been the nexus it has provided for a variety of family therapy approaches that concern themselves primarily with modifying problematic patterns of family communication.

The Eastern Seaboard

The form and pattern of the experimentation and discoveries that characterized the eastern seaboard in the early 1950s were decidedly different from those conducted on the west coast by the Palo Alto group. While a number of the significant eastern investigators intersected with one another, the majority of their developing ideas emerged independently. In addition, while psychiatry was clearly in a subordinate role on the west coast, a majority of the early experimenters on the eastern seaboard were psychiatrists with traditional psychoanalytic training. Finally, while the Palo Alto group worked deductively by applying theory from the social and behavioral sciences to clinical phenomena, the findings on the east coast were formulated inductively through repeated observations of clinical families.

John Bell, psychology professor at Clark University in the 1950s (ironically where Freud gave his introductory lectures), is frequently identified as being the first family therapist (Broderick & Schrader, 1981; Olson, 1971). His discovery of the therapeutic effects of seeing the whole family together, however, as reported in the *Saturday Evening Post* (Silverman & Silverman, 1982), was rather serendipitous. He reported that after he "heard" a British colleague tell him in 1951 of John Bowlby's practice of interviewing all of the members of a patient's family, he began to meet regularly with the family of a 13-year-old adolescent referred to him for behavioral problems. It was only after Bell observed a relationship between the acting-out problems of the adolescent and the patterns of family interaction that he realized he had misunderstood his British colleague. Indeed, the practice of seeing the family as a group was not employed by Bowlby at all; rather, his methodology consisted of seeing each family member in individual sessions (Broderick & Schrader, 1981). Unfortunately Bell's observations and experiences with this family were not published, since there were few available journals seeking such reports at the time. Like the discoveries of some of the other pioneers, his efforts were reported only in rather informal professional circles.

Nathan Ackerman and Murray Bowen, two of the most influential of the east coast pioneers, were both classically trained psychiatrists who at separate times were affiliated with the prestigious Menninger Clinic of Topeka, Kansas. When Ackerman came to the clinic in the 1930s, he previously had been involved in the study of the emotional problems of unemployed miners in western Pennsylvania. He was struck by the similar symptoms that characterized the families of these men and concluded that "family life was radically altered by the miner's inability to fulfill his habitual role as provider" (Ackerman, 1967, p. 126). Although his work at Menninger generally was characterized by adherence to the psychiatric principle of individual professionals for each family member, he utilized his private practice for experimentation with his evolving interest in family dynamics.

By the late 1940s and early 1950s, however, Ackerman began to try out his independent discoveries within the framework of the clinic and began to send his staff on home visits to study patterns of family interaction (Guerin, 1976). He also conducted seminars about the relationship between the diagnosis of children and particular patterns of parenting (Broderick & Schrader, 1981). Ackerman's central contribution to the theory of family therapy emerged from his view of the family as a dynamic organism. His approach to treatment emphasized the notion that there is a constant process of exchange and reciprocity transpiring between the person, his family, and society at large (Foley, 1974). Although he wrote about his ideas with clarity and frequency (Ackerman, 1938, 1958, 1961, 1966, 1972), his primary contribution to the development of the family therapy movement was one more of statesmanship and advocacy than of conceptual development. For many years he was seen as a bridge between the psychoanalytically oriented medical community and those proposing models of family interaction that contradicted or were not compatible with traditional psychodynamic theory.

Murray Bowen, the other Menninger pioneer, had developed a special interest in the treatment of psychotic children. Like many of his peers, he spent the early part of his career examining and treating the apparent symbiotic bond that appeared to characterize the maternal relationships of schizophrenic children. In 1951 he began inviting the mothers and shortly thereafter the fathers of schizophrenic patients to enter into a live-in arrangement at the clinic. While he made some observations about the entire family, his primary focus at this point remained with the mother and child (Guerin, 1976).

Upon leaving Menninger and joining the staff of the National Institute of Mental Health in Washington, Bowen widened his conceptual lens to include the whole family. In what was one of the most revolutionary psychiatric research projects of all time, he began to hospitalize the entire families of identified schizophrenic patients. Although in the beginning each family member was assigned a separate therapist, as his thinking about the client system of family therapy became more clear, Bowen began to assign each family to only one therapist. While the project was to experience financial and administrative difficulties in the late 1950s and eventually to dissolve, it gave birth to the most complete theoretical statement of the process by which dysfunction in families may be transmitted down and across generations.

When Bowen left the directorship of the family section at NIMH to go to Georgetown University, he was replaced by Lyman Wynne. In addition to a medical degree, Wynne earned a Ph.D. in social relations and was schooled from the beginning in understanding both research and the influences of social determinants on human behavior. Prior to coming to NIMH he worked therapeutically with families of patients at Massachusetts General Hospital, and before replacing Bowen in the family section he did clinical work at Prince Georges County, Maryland Mental Health Clinic (Broderick & Schrader, 1981). Sensitized to the work of Talcott Parsons early in his career, it was at this time that Wynne began to formulate his thoughts on the family structure of schizophrenic families. He was one of the first researchers to describe the artificiality of both positive (pseudomutuality) and negative (pseudohostility) emotions in families with a severely disturbed member. These observations provided the foundation for a subsequent theory of family structure and schizophrenia (Wynne, Ryckoff, Day, & Hirsch, 1958). During the late 1950s Wynne also was instrumental in establishing linkages with the Palo Alto group, and in 1960 he began exchanging video tapes of family therapy sessions with Don Jackson.

Although the reverberations of their work were not to be felt until the mid to late 1960s, the interdisciplinary practitioners and researchers brought together at the Eastern Pennsylvania Psychiatric Institute in Philadelphia by Ivan Boszormenyi-Nagy in the late 1950s made a lasting impact on the development of family treatment. Nagy, an analytically trained psychiatrist, attracted such noted social scientists as Ray Birdwhistle and Al Scheflen to join his project investigating the relationship between family interaction and schizophrenia. These researchers extended their study of the schizophrenic process to the homes of families with schizophrenic members. As a group they became particularly concerned with the social and environmental processes of schizophrenia. This early work was to lead to a number of significant contributions, among them two particularly important intergenerational approaches to family therapy: Boszormenyi-Nagy and Spark's contextual family therapy (1973) and James Framo's family-of-origin approach to couples therapy (1976).

The final founding parent, Carl Whitaker, has become known as the most unconventional among the unconventional. Although it has been suggested that he may have convened the first meeting of the family therapy movement in 1953 (Broderick & Schrader, 1981), his highly individualistic therapeutic technique makes his work difficult to describe and replicate. In 1946, after having experimented briefly with both cotherapy and whole-family sessions in private practice in Oakridge, Tennessee, Whitaker became Chairman of the Department of Psychiatry at Emory University in Atlanta, Georgia. Here he pioneered such presently institutionalized practices as observing family members behind one-way mirrors, live supervision, and impromptu case conferences that interrupted the process of therapy. Although Whitaker has provided the family movement with a host of theoretical ideas about family interaction and therapy (Whitaker & Keith, 1981; Whitaker & Malone, 1953), perhaps his greatest contribution has been his therapeutic style. He was the first and continues to be the most dramatic representative of the idea that the family therapist is an action-oriented—indeed, provocative—agent of change.

The Development of Family Therapy

The researchers and practitioners of the 1950s were held together only by a rather loosely organized informal "underground" network of privately arranged visitations and personal communications. It was not until the 1957 annual meeting of the American Orthopsychiatric Association that the first national meeting of family therapists and researchers was held. Bowen cites this meeting as the beginning of family therapy on a "national level" (1975, p. 369). He sees this and the subsequent May 1957 family section meeting of the American Psychiatric Association as (1) providing initial awareness among the earlier pioneers of the potential of the growing movement and (2) launching the family practice careers of many more inexperienced therapists.

David Olson described the following decade, the 1960s, as one of childhood and adolescence for the family therapy movement (Olson et al., 1980). Clearly it was during this decade that the early founders discovered they were not alone. This 10-year span saw the emergence of more formalized collaboration, the expanded dissemination of ideas through the literature, and the emergence of a truly national family therapy professional community.

One of the more instrumental forces in forging the commonality within the movement during the decade was the young psychiatrist Donald Jackson. Although the Bateson project did not end until 1962, by 1959 Jackson had founded the Mental Research Institute in Palo Alto and, with Ackerman in 1961, had cofounded *Family Process*, the first professional journal devoted exclusively to family theory, therapy, and research. Both institutions continue to this day and are among the most influential and prestigious vehicles in the family therapy movement's knowledge-development, information-dissemination, and training enterprises.

As a psychiatrist, Jackson was more concerned than was anthropologist Bateson with the application of the double-bind communications research to clinical work with troubled families. Indeed, the development of family therapy was the primary concern of the Mental Research Institute; interestingly, the emergent contributors to the literature of family therapy of the 1960s all had direct or indirect links with Jackson and the Institute.

Virginia Satir

According to Guerin, Virginia Satir, a psychiatric social worker affiliated with the Chicago Psychiatric Institute, became interested in the work of Bowen and his NIMH project, described previously (Guerin, 1976). By 1959 she had met Bowen, who suggested she seek out Jackson at MRI. The two (Jackson and Satir) formed an immediate professional affiliation based on their joint interest in patterns of family communication, and Satir began working at MRI that same year. Here she joined them in the active elaboration and testing of those ideas. She says of her affiliation with MRI, "I worked on a systems approach long before I understood anything about it and before I ever heard a name for it. Then in 1957 I read Don Jackson's article 'Toward a Theory of Schizophrenia,' and I began to know what was going on" (Satir, Stachowiak, & Taschman, 1975, p. 165).

One of Satir's greatest gifts was her ability both to interpret and to render practical, relatively complex formulations. Her publication in 1964 of *Conjoint Family Therapy* was a benchmark in the dissemination of family therapy as a method. While it expressed her unique point of view about helping troubled families, it also translated and disseminated to the general public many of the ideas pioneered at MRI in the early 1960s.

Following the publication of *Conjoint Family Therapy*, Satir left MRI to become the first director of the Esalen Institute in Big Sur, California. At that time Esalen was gaining national prominence as the leading teaching/training facility for humanistic psychology. The focus at Esalen on growth, awareness, and feeling was particularly congruent with Satir's emerging interest in sensory processes. In her subsequent publications (Satir, 1967, 1972; Satir et al., 1975; Bandler, Grinder, & Satir, 1976) she was to integrate her MRI-nurtured communications ideas with the premises of growth-oriented psychologies.

Satir's influence grew immensely during the 1960s, and she clearly was viewed as one of the foremost leaders in the field. While her work reflects an eclectic mixture of ideas that range across a variety of systems of thought, her more recent work identifies four major concepts, all of which become targets of her therapeutic action system: (1) the self-esteem of the individual family member; (2) the quality, channels, and patterning of family communication; (3) the rules that regulate the family's behavior and affective expression; and (4) the linkages by which the members of the family unit relate to the society at large and to its institutions (Satir, 1972).

Jay Haley

When the Bateson project was terminated in 1962, Jay Haley joined Jackson and Satir at MRI. While he shared his colleagues' fascination with the process of human communication and the application of these ideas to patterns of family interaction, he also became involved in more individualized areas of research in which he has made cumulative contributions since the early 1960s. A major area of interest, the common threads that cut across all types of psychotherapy, resulted in the publication of his first book shortly after he began his formal association with MRI. In this volume, *The Strategies of Psychotherapy* (1963), Haley argued that, regardless of theoretical orientation, the therapeutic encounter always was characterized by a paradoxical situation, the understanding and management of which leads to effective therapy. He suggested that, while the therapist establishes a benevolent framework in which change is to transpire, the therapist also allows the client to continue with *unchanged behavior* and permits this paradox to continue as long as the behavior remains unchanged (Haley, 1963, p. 181).

The search for generic properties among therapies as well as his early experiences with the Bateson project uniquely equipped Haley for this informal role as chronicler of and spokesman for the family therapy movement in the 1960s. Indeed, when Jackson and Ackerman founded *Family Process* in 1961, Haley was selected as the first editor, a role he carried throughout the decade.

Haley's concern with the common threads of psychotherapy in general and its paradoxical nature in particular set the stage for work toward the development of his own particular approach to family therapy. This approach was to become known as Strategic Family Therapy a decade later (Madanes & Haley, 1977). A number of distinguishing characteristics of Haley's therapy have been noted previously (Haley, 1971, 1976, 1980). The most salient characteristic, however, was his concern with the nature of the hierarchical arrangement of family relationships. Indeed, the clarity of the rules governing the family hierarchy was the most significant indicator of family health. Consequently, the goals of therapy, defining and changing the family hierarchy, were achieved through a therapeutic power struggle characterized by the therapist's purposeful selection and implementation of interventive strategies. Why change takes place or how symptoms developed were unimportant to Haley; consequently, unlike the work of Satir, the family members' insight, awareness, or knowledge of how the family system operates were not relevant to the process of therapy.

Salvadore Minuchin

Haley left MRI in the mid 1960s to join Salvadore Minuchin at the Philadelphia Child Guidance Clinic. Like Haley, Minuchin also recently had completed a research project that left him questioning traditional notions about the role of insight, understanding, and the expression of feeling in the process of therapeutic change. Minuchin's project, however, unlike Haley's and the majority of early family interaction investigations, did not focus on schizophrenics and their families. Rather, Minuchin and his colleagues on the Wiltwyck School Project worked with young black and Puerto Rican adolescents from New York City ghettos. While they began their research with no working hypotheses, the purpose of the research project was to shed light on the dynamics of disadvantaged, "hard-core" families that had produced more than one acting-out or delinquent child (Minuchin, Montalvo, Guerney, Rosman, & Shumer, 1967). As a result of this project Minuchin and his colleagues concluded that the most important factor determining the patterns of interaction in such a family was its structure, and that the boundaries, alignments of subsystems, and distribution of power within the family were the critical elements defining family health or pathology.

Following the Wiltwyck School Project, Minuchin was joined in Philadelphia by two of his colleagues, Braulio Montalvo and Bernice Rosman, where, with the help of Haley, they developed the Structural Model of Family Therapy and transformed the Philadelphia Child Guidance Clinic into an internationally renowned family therapy treatment, training, and research center. Although Haley left in the mid 1970s to develop further his Strategic Family Therapy, Minuchin remained at the clinic, where he continued to refine the tenets of the structural approach (Minuchin, 1974; Minuchin & Fishman, 1981).

The Growth of Family Therapy

Following the discoveries of the 1950s and the operationalizations of family therapy in the 1960s, the family therapy movement grew in an unprecedented fashion. Its growth may be observed with regard to the range of problems to which it is presently applied, the number of practitioners and their involvement in professional organizations, the body of literature that it has produced, and the development of its training enterprise.

Range of Problems

Although the idea of family therapy had its origins in the study and treatment of schizophrenia and juvenile delinquency, the theories of family interaction that have emerged from those areas have been expanded, modified, and transformed to be applicable to the full range of problems. While family therapy continues to be viewed as a treatment of choice for families with a schizophrenic member (McFarlane, 1983), many of its premises and treatment procedures have been prescribed and applied to related psychotic disorders (Keith & Whitaker, 1982). In addition, at the other end of the diagnostic continuum, family-oriented approaches are advocated for the enrichment and restoration of a variety of family and organizational relationships (L'Abate, 1981), as well as for such diverse mid-range emotional and behavioral problems as juvenile delinquency (Alexander & Parsons, 1973; Klein, Alexander, & Parsons, 1977), drug and alcohol abuse (Stanton & Todd, 1979; Steinglass, 1976), physical illness (Haley, 1973; Weakland, 1977), emotional disturbances of children and adults (Garrigan & Bambrick, 1977; Nelson, 1983), and of course the general adjustment problems of marriage and parent/child relationships (Guerney, 1977; Paolino & McCrady, 1978).

Practitioners and Professional Organizations

Since the practice of family therapy cuts across all of the mental health professions, attempts to estimate the number of practitioners oriented to a family approach to treatment must be approached with caution. Although the field has yet to produce a comprehensive inventory of its practitioners, Hansen and L'Abate have estimated that approximately 40,000 professionals either "claim or desire" the label family therapist (1982, p. 295). They provide, however, no source for the development of their estimate. When one compares Hansen and L'Abate's estimate with Zuk's early surveys estimating a mere 500 practitioners in 1967 and from 1000 to 1200 in 1971 (Zuk, 1967, 1971), the growth of the field is truly unprecedented in the mental health enterprise.

The growth of membership in family therapy professional organizations can be catalogued more accurately. Three organizations predominate: the American Association for Marital and Family Therapy (AAMFT), the Marital and Family Therapy Section of the National Council on Family Relations, and the American Family Therapy Association (AFTA). AAMFT, the largest of the professional organizations, probably includes about one-fourth of all family therapists (Hansen & L'Abate, 1982, p. 295). The 1983 membership list includes over

10,300 members, 1300 of whom are in associate or nonpracticing membership categories. The growth of this organization is staggering when one considers the 1967 membership list included but 973 persons.

The National Council on Family Relations is the nation's oldest continuing organization concerned with the quality of family life. Its membership is divided into a number of different sections reflecting a wide range of interests. The Marital and Family Therapy Section, first organized as a marital counseling interest group, is presently (1984) comprised of over 900 members. AFTA is the youngest and the smallest of the family therapy professional organizations. It was founded in 1977 by a group of *Family Process* editors and friends and listed 150 charter members in that year. Since that time its membership has grown to over 700 professionals, many of whom are among the most powerful and prestigious in the family therapy movement.

Publications

In 1958, when Nathan Ackerman first published the *Psychodynamics of Family Life,* it was the first book devoted entirely to the diagnosis and treatment of family relationships. Similarly, in 1961, when Don Jackson joined with Ackerman to found *Family Process,* it was the only journal in the field devoted exclusively to family theory and therapy. Since that time the field has literally exploded with both books and journals. During the decade of the 1970s alone there were over 200 books on family therapy published representing the range of helping disciplines (Olson et al., 1980), and Framo and Green's (1980) historical biography lists almost 400 different books and reference volumes. There are at the present time almost a dozen different English-language family therapy journals and an equal number of journals published in foreign languages.

Training

In 1955, training in family therapy was being provided to but a handful of individuals at five locations distributed across the continental United States. By 1980, survey data collected by Bloch and Weiss (1981) suggested that family therapists were being trained at 175 different centers distributed across the country and including Europe, Canada, Mexico, and Australia. These centers, including the traditional academic and professional departments of psychology, psychiatry, and social work, also are including newer interdisciplinary programs in marital and family therapy as well as using the services of private free-standing institutes. Bloch and Weiss also estimated the total number of students who were enrolled in long-term training (one to three years) in these various centers during 1979–1980 to be over 4000. In addition, the family therapy training enterprise is supplemented by workshops and family therapy enrichment programs for practicing professionals. Bloch and Weiss estimated over 18,000 persons attended these workshops during 1979–1980. Recognizing that considerable overlap exists between the enrichment programs and enrollees in long-term training, the authors estimated that almost 10,000 persons participated in some form of family therapy training in 1979–1980.

Summary

In this chapter we have highlighted the development and growth of the field of family therapy from its origins in the middle of the twentieth century to the present time. We discussed how the idea of treating the whole family had its origins in a number of locales distributed across the continental United States and how this idea was "stumbled upon," experimented with, and/or discovered simultaneously by a number of different mental health professionals. In so doing we have referenced selectively what we consider to be the significant benchmarks in the birth of the interdisciplinary profession of family therapy: individuals and ideas that have provided the nexus and the identity of a new way of viewing and treating human behavior. Finally, we have attempted to acquaint the reader with the magnitude of the impact of the family therapy movement on the mental health enterprise by reviewing available quantitative indices of its growth and development. As the family therapy movement continued to grow in the 1960s and beyond, so too did it begin to diversify as new and varied conceptualizations of family life and functioning were assigned differential importance in guiding the clinical enterprise. It is toward a closer analysis of this diversification process that we turn in the next chapter.

References

Abt, L. E., & Stuart, I. R. (Eds.). *The new therapies.* New York: Van Nostrand, 1982.
Ackerman, N. The unity of the family. *Archives of Pediatrics*, 1938, *55*, 51–62.
Ackerman, N. *The psychodynamics of family life.* New York: Basic Books, 1958.

Ackerman, N. A dynamic framework of the clinical approach to family conflict. In N. Ackerman, F. Beatman, & S. Sherman (Eds.), *Exploring the base for family therapy.* New York: Jewish Family Services, 1961.

Ackerman, N. *Treating the troubled family.* New York: Basic Books, 1966.

Ackerman, N. The emergence of family diagnosis and treatment: A personal view. *Psychotherapy,* 1967, *4,* 125–129.

Ackerman, N. The growing edge of family therapy. In C. Sager & H. Kaplan (Eds.), *Progress in group and family therapy.* New York: Brunner/Mazel, 1972.

Alexander, J., & Parsons, B. Short-term behavioral intervention with delinquent families: Impact on family process and recidivism. *Journal of Abnormal Psychology,* 1973, *81,* 219–225.

Andolfi, M. Paradox in psychotherapy. *American Journal of Psychoanalysis,* 1974, *34,* 221–228.

Bandler, R., Grinder, J., & Satir, V. *Changing with families.* Palo Alto, Calif.: Science and Behavior Books, 1976.

Bateson, G. *Steps to an ecology of mind.* New York: Ballantine, 1972.

Bateson, G., Jackson, D. D., Haley, J., & Weakland, J. H. Toward a theory of schizophrenia. *Behavioral Science,* 1956, *1,* 251–264.

Berger, A. A test of the double bind hypothesis of schizophrenia. *Family Process,* 1965, *4,* 198–205.

Berger, M. M. (Ed.). *Beyond the double bind.* New York: Brunner/Mazel, 1978.

Bloch, D. A., & Weiss, H. M. Training facilities in marital and family therapy. *Family Process,* 1981, *20,* 133–146.

Boszormenyi-Nagy, I., & Spark, G. *Invisible loyalties: Reciprocity in intergenerational family therapy.* New York: Harper & Row, 1973.

Bowen, M. Family therapy after twenty years. In D. X. Freedman & J. E. Dyrud (Eds.), *American handbook of psychiatry* (vol. 5). New York: Basic Books, 1975.

Broderick, C. B., & Schrader, S. S. The history of professional marriage and family therapy. In A. S. Gurman & D. P. Kniskern (Eds.), *Handbook of family therapy.* New York: Brunner/Mazel, 1981.

Bucher, R., & Strauss, A. Professions in progress. *American Journal of Sociology,* 1961, *66,* 325–334.

Carlton, T. O. Social work as a profession in process. *Journal of Social Welfare,* 1977, *4,* 15–25.

Flugel, J. C. *The psycho-analytic study of the family.* London: Hogarth Press, 1931.

Foley, V. D. *An introduction to family therapy.* New York: Grune and Stratton, 1974.

Framo, J. L. Family origin as a therapeutic resource for adults in marital and family therapy: You can and should go home again. *Family Process,* 1976, *15,* 193–210.

Framo, J. L., & Green, R. J. *Bibliography of books related to family and marital systems theory and therapy.* Upland, Calif.: American Association for Marital and Family Therapy, 1980.

Garrigan, J. J., & Bambrick, A. F. Family therapy for disturbed children. *Journal of Marriage and Family Counseling,* 1977, *3,* 83–93.

Goldfried, M. R. (Ed.). *Converging themes in psychotherapy: Trends in psychodynamic, humanistic and behavioral practice.* New York: Springer, 1982.

Guerin, P. J. (Ed.). *Family therapy: Theory and practice.* New York: Gardner Press, 1976.

Guerney, B. *Relationship enhancement.* San Francisco: Jossey-Bass, 1979.

Gurman, A. S., & Kniskern, D. P. (Eds.). *Handbook of family therapy.* New York: Brunner/Mazel, 1981.

Haley, J. *The strategies of psychotherapy.* New York: Grune and Stratton, 1963.

Haley, J. *Changing families.* New York: Grune and Stratton, 1971.

Haley, J. *Uncommon therapy.* New York: W. W. Norton, 1973.

Haley, J. *Problem-solving therapy.* San Francisco: Jossey-Bass, 1976.

Haley, J. *Leaving home.* New York: McGraw-Hill, 1980.

Hansen, J. C., & L'Abate, L. *Approaches to family therapy.* New York: Macmillan, 1982.

Hoffman, L. *Foundations of family therapy.* New York: Basic Books, 1981.

Kaslow, F. W. (Ed.). *The international book of family therapy.* New York: Brunner/Mazel, 1982.

Keith, D. V., & Whitaker, C. Experiential/symbolic family therapy. In A. M. Horne & M. M. Ohlsen (Eds.), *Family counseling and therapy.* Itasca, Ill.: R. E. Peacock, 1982.

Klein, N. C., Alexander, J. F., & Parsons, B. V. Impact of family systems intervention on recidivism and sibling delinquency: A model of primary prevention and program evaluation. *Journal of Consulting and Clinical Psychology,* 1977, *45,* 469–474.

Kuhn, T. *The structure of scientific revolutions.* Chicago: The University of Chicago Press, 1970.

L'Abate, L. Skill training programs for couples and families. In A. S. Gurman & D. P. Kniskern (Eds.), *Handbook of family therapy.* New York: Brunner/Mazel, 1981.

Liddle, H. A. On the problem of eclecticism: A call for epistemologic clarification and human scale theories. *Family Process,* 1982, *21,* 243–250.

Madanes, C., & Haley, J. Dimensions of family therapy. *Journal of Nervous and Mental Disease,* 1977, *165,* 88–98.

McFarlane, W. R. (Ed.). *Family therapy in schizophrenia.* New York: Guilford Press, 1983.

Minuchin, S. *Families and family therapy.* Cambridge: Harvard University Press, 1974.

Minuchin, S., & Fishman, H. *Family therapy techniques.* Cambridge: Harvard University Press, 1981.

Minuchin, S., Montalvo, B., Guerney, B. G., Rosman, B. L., & Schumer, F. *Families of the slums.* New York: Basic Books, 1967.

Nelson, J. C. *Family treatment.* Englewood Cliffs, N.J.: Prentice-Hall, 1983.

Olson, D. H. Marital and family therapy: Integrative review and critique. In C.

B. Broderick (Ed.), *A decade of family research and action.* Minneapolis: National Council on Family Relations, 1971.

Olson, D. H. Empirically unbinding the double bind. *Family Process*, 1982, *11*, 69–93.

Olson, D. H., Russell, C. S., & Sprenkle, D. H. Marital and family therapy: A decade review. *Journal of Marriage and the Family*, 1980, *42*, 973–994.

Paolino, T. J., & McCrady, B. S. (Eds.). *Marriage and marital therapy: Psychoanalytic, behavioral and systems theory perspectives.* New York: Brunner/Mazel, 1978.

Parloff, M. B. Can psychotherapy research guide the policymaker? A little knowledge may be a dangerous thing. *American Psychologist*, 1979, *3*, 296–306.

Rich, M. E. *A belief in people: A history of family social work.* New York: Family Service Association of America, 1956.

Richmond, M. E. *Social diagnosis.* New York: Russell Sage, 1917.

Satir, V. *Conjoint family therapy.* Palo Alto, Calif.: Science and Behavior Books, 1964.

Satir, V. A family of angels. In J. Haley & L. Hoffman (Eds.), *Techniques of family therapy.* New York: Basic Books, 1967.

Satir, V. *Peoplemaking.* Palo Alto, Calif.: Science and Behavior Books, 1972.

Satir, V., Stachowiak, J., & Taschman, H. A. *Helping families to change.* New York: Jason Aronson, 1975.

Schaefer, R. *A new language for psychoanalysis.* New Haven: Yale University Press, 1976.

Silverman, M., & Silverman, M. Psychiatry inside the family circle. *Saturday Evening Post*, November, 1982, 46–51.

Simon, R. Conclusion of an interview with Salvador Minuchin. *Family Therapy Practice Network Newsletter*, 1980, *3*, 5–10.

Sluzki, E. E., & Veron, E. The double bind as a universal pathogenic situation. *Family Process*, 1971, *10*, 397–409.

Smith, Z. D. *Proceedings of the National Conference in Charities and Corrections.* New York: National Conference in Charities and Corrections, 1890.

Stanton, M. D., & Todd, T. C. Structural family therapy with drug addicts. In E. Kaufman & P. Kaufman (Eds.), *The family therapy of drug and alcohol abuse.* New York: Gardner Press, 1979.

Steinglass, P. Experimenting with family treatment approaches to alcoholism, 1950–1975. *Family Process*, 1976, *15*, 97–124.

Vollmer, H., & Mills, D. (Eds.). *Professionalization.* Englewood Cliffs, N.J.: Prentice Hall, 1966.

Warriner, C. K. Groups are real: A reaffirmation. *American Sociological Review*, 1956, *21*, 549–554.

Watzlawick, P., Weakland, J., & Fisch, R. Change: Principles of problem formation and problem resolution. New York: W. W. Norton, 1974.

Weakland, J. H. Family somatics: A neglected edge. *Family Process*, 1978, *16*, 263–272.

Weakland, J. H., & Fry, W. Letters of mothers of schizophrenics. *American Journal of Orthopsychiatry*, 1962, 32, 604–623.

Weeks, G. R., & L'Abate, L. *Paradoxical psychotherapy: Theory and practice with individuals, couples, and families.* New York: Brunner/Mazel, 1982.

Whitaker, C. A. (Ed.). *Psychotherapy of chronic schizophrenic patients.* Boston: Little, Brown, 1958.

Whitaker, C., & Keith, D. Symbolic-experiential family therapy. In A. S. Gurman & D. P. Kniskern (Eds.), *Handbook of family therapy.* New York: Brunner/Mazel, 1981.

Whitaker, C. A., & Malone, T. P. *The roots of psychotherapy.* New York: Blakiston, 1953.

Whitehead, A. N., & Russell, B. *Principia mathematica.* Cambridge: Cambridge University Press, 1910.

Wynne, L. C., Ryckoff, I., Day, J., & Hirsch, S. Pseudomutuality in the family relations of schizophrenics. *Psychiatry*, 1958, 21, 205–220.

Zuk, G. H. A listing of therapists doing family therapy. *Pastoral Psychology*, 1967, 3, 16–19.

Zuk, G. H. Family therapy during 1964–1970. *Psychotherapy: Theory, Research and Practice*, 1971, 8, 90–97.

2

The Classification of the Family Therapies

As we suggested in Chapter 1, the nature of the growth of family therapy practice can be expected to conform to a paradoxical dynamic that has typified the development of other professions and the theories employed by their constituent professionals. Indeed, as family therapists have joined together collaboratively to advance the knowledge frontiers of areas of mutual concern, their efforts also have produced within-group divergence with regard to the practice of family therapy.

As the profession has grown and as this branching process has transpired, family therapists have made periodic attempts to identify and classify the emerging field with regard to the therapeutic issues on which the various family therapies converge and those on which they diverge. Historically these attempts have utilized the same two dimensions of therapeutic practice that have been employed to order the individual-oriented psychotherapies. The first dimension, *belief systems*, classifies therapists with regard to variations in their assumptions about human behavior and the process of therapy. The second dimension, *therapeutic action systems,* describes the differences among therapists with regard to what they actually do and how they do it during the process of therapy (Sundland, 1977; Wallach & Strupp, 1964).

However, since family therapy grew and developed inductively, equal attention has not been given to each of these dimensions. Rather, the early attempts to classify the emerging approaches to family practice (the efforts of the 1960s) focused almost exclusively on action systems by accentuating differences in therapeutic style (Haley, 1962) and the presumed effects of personality on style (Beels & Ferber, 1969). Paralleling the unprecedented growth of the movement itself in the 1970s and the increased number of outlets for professional publication, greater attention was directed to the varying belief systems among the emerging forms of family therapy. During the present decade, typologies have tended to emphasize neither action nor belief systems exclusively. Rather, the organizing focus generally has been the school, model, or approach as viewed by varying interpreters of the field. To provide the background for our study, therefore, in this chapter we will review chronologically the literature of the field, beginning with the earliest attempts to profile action systems of family therapists in the 1960s and concluding with more recent attempts to order the field with regard to models, schools, or larger, more inclusive constructs.

The 1960s: Action Systems

Perhaps the first attempt to describe the growing field of family therapy appeared in the initial issue of *Family Process*, in an article by its first editor, Jay Haley (1962). Utilizing the satire and paradox that have characterized many of his subsequent writings on family therapy, Haley humorously defined nine schools with reference to nine significant pioneers. The first three schools addressed themselves to the more moderately disturbed families. The Dignified School of Family Therapy (John Bell) was distinguished by its adherents' refusal to side with particular family members. The therapist attempted to arbitrate and understand the source of family conflict through careful listening and negotiation. Haley described the second school as the Dynamic Psychodynamic School of Family Diagnosis, an obvious reference to Nathan Ackerman and his associates. In counterdistinction to the first school, this school advocated the side-taking function and actively pursued that end with many different family members. Haley's characterization of the final school concerned with moderately disturbed families was dubbed the Chuck It and Run School. The obvious reference here was Charles Fulweiler and the growing tendency among some family therapists to stimulate conflict among family members, leave the consultation room, and observe the conflict resolution strategies (or the absence of same) through one-way mirrors or recording devices.

Haley identified two schools that focused on the more severely disturbed family by contrasting the styles of Virginia Satir (Great Mother's School) with that of her former colleague at MRI, Don Jackson. In regard to Satir, Haley emphasized the individual acceptance and nurturance of family members that was carried out in the attempt to create a network of more trusting intrafamily relationships, while he stereotyped Jackson's work (Stonewall School of Family Therapy) by portraying the therapist's use of paradox and system provocation.

The final four schools and their representative therapists were catalogued as the "multiplication schools." This distinction reflected the then-emerging experimentation with two or more therapists. The first of these, the Eyebrows School, targeted the work of R. D. Laing and other British family therapists concerned with the subjectivity of the family members' interpretation of reality and the use of dual therapists in order to understand better the inner world of family members. The Brotherly Love School attempted to portray the team visiting of families in their homes by interdisciplinary staff of the Eastern Pennsylvania Psychiatric Institute in Philadelphia; while the third multiplication school, the Total Push in the Tall Country School, satirized the assignment of different family therapists to each family member, a procedure then characteristic of Robert MacGregor's multiple impact therapy being developed in Texas. With the final multiplication school, Hospitalize the Whole Damn Maelstrom, Haley attempted to describe Murray Bowen's early experimentation with the hospitalization of entire families with a schizophrenic member.

It was not until the 1960s came to a close, some eight years after Haley's initial "attempt," that the first systematic effort to classify the family therapies was reported. From a content analysis of the literature, a review of video tapes, and extensive personal exposure to the work of the field's most distinguished practitioners, Beels and Ferber (1969) concluded that the therapist's personality (and consequently what he or she does) was the clearest available criterion for classifying the family therapies. As they surveyed the field they suggested that belief systems about family therapy were often *a posteriori* rationalizations for the practice of the therapy itself.

By focusing on therapeutic presence or use of self within the family treatment session, two personality types emerged from their inductive analysis. One group, labeled as conductors by Beels and Ferber (1969), seemed to have more vigorous personalities:

> They . . . can hold audiences spellbound by their talks and demonstrations. They have a keen, explicit sense of their own values and

> goals which they, in one way or another, hope to get the families to adopt. Some of them are regarded by their critics as sadistic, manipulative, exhibitionistic and insensitive. [p. 286]

Obviously, within the treatment sessions these conductors were in complete command. Their therapeutic style was characterized by personal dominance, and they tended to focus on the elder's side of family generational hierarchy. They established their seniority early in the treatment session and continued to stay there.

The second category of therapists, the reactors, on the other hand, were described as less compelling public personalities:

> They present themselves to the families not only as themselves but in various roles dictated by the tactics or by the group dynamics of the family. They refer often in their writings of the danger of being swamped, confused, inveigled or excluded by families. They have goals and values, but they are more likely to be . . . a secret agenda in therapy. [Beels & Ferber, 1969, p. 286]

Interestingly, only the reactors were linked with particular belief systems. Within this group, Beels and Ferber created an additional dichotomous distinction in relation to the content to which therapists react. The first group, the "systems purists," tended to observe less traditional psychiatric phenomena than did their reactor counterparts, the "analysts." The systems purists observed and responded to patterns of interpersonal influence and to implicit and explicit rules that regulated this influence. They were minimally concerned with the intrapsychic functioning of individual family members and quite indifferent to the analysis of motivation. The analysts, on the other hand, tended to make family observations in the psychodynamic tradition and consequently were very much concerned with internal processes of each of the family members. They used diagnostic procedures and terms that made it appear they were conducting individual therapy in a group setting.

Beels and Ferber (1969) continued their analysis by describing the therapies of 15 different family therapists and their associates. Table 2–1 lists the conductors and reactors as identified by Beels and Ferber and also divides the reactors into systems purists and analysts. While Beels and Ferber's work certainly provided some order to the field, it is rather unclear why they did not attempt to distinguish among the conductors. While these therapists certainly tend to converge with respect to the dominance of their personalities, a glance at the table

TABLE 2-1   Beels and Ferber's View of the Field of Family Therapy
in 1969: Conductors and Reactors.

	Reactors	
Conductors	*Systems Purists*	*Analysts*
N. Ackerman	J. Haley	I. Boszormenyi-Nagy
J. Bell	D. Jackson	J. Framo
M. Bowen	G. Zuk	C. Whitaker
R. MacGregor		L. Wynne
S. Minuchin		
N. Paul		
V. Satir		
R. Tharp		

Source: C. C. Beels and A. Ferber, Family Therapy: A view. *Family Process*, 1969, *8*,
280–332.

informs even the casual observer of the family therapy field that there
are certainly as many observable differences among the conductors as
among the reactors.

The 1970s: Belief Systems

Nathan Ackerman set the tone for the attempts to classify the family
therapies in the 1970s. In one of his final analyses of the field before his
untimely death in 1971, he wrote,

> The most striking feature of our field today is the emergence of a bewilder-
> ing array of diverse forms of family treatment. Each therapist seems to be
> doing his own thing. We are faced squarely with a challenge to evaluate
> this diversity. Which of the differences are real? Which more apparent
> than real? Does the dramatic quality of these differences, in effect,
> obscure their basic sameness? [Ackerman, 1970, p. 123]

Indeed, by 1970 it was clear to many observers that the differences
between the therapies might go beyond the personalities and styles of
the leading figures in the field and that they might reflect different
assumptions about family interaction and therapy. As Haley (1968, p.
151) pointed out, practitioners during the 1960s struggled to find a
theory to fit their practice. As the new decade began, greater interest
developed in building theory that could guide rather than conform to
practice with families.

In 1970 the Group for the Advancement of Psychiatry (GAP) published a report describing the theoretical orientations of family therapists attending meetings of the American Orthopsychiatric Association in 1965 and 1966. The data collected were gathered by questionnaire from almost 300 respondents representing the disciplines of psychiatry, psychology, social work, nursing, the ministry, and sociology. Almost 80 percent of the family therapists, however, were from psychiatry, psychology, or social work, with the latter group comprising the most frequently represented profession (40%).

Two findings were particularly pertinent. The first was in regard to the family theorists whom the respondents viewed as "most influential" to their practice, while the second described the belief and action systems reported by the respondents to characterize their practice. Of the 21 theorists reported by the respondents as influencing their own practice with families, the most highly ranked were Virginia Satir, Nathan Ackerman, and Don Jackson, followed by Jay Haley and Murray Bowen. Additionally, and perhaps illustrating the lack of a strong national affiliation with the family therapy movement as a whole, the respondents' choices tended to be influenced by the geographical accessibility of theorists. Respondents on the west coast tended to rank Satir, Jackson, and Haley high, while those from the east tended to prefer Bowen and Ackerman.

To provide data in regard to belief and action systems, the therapists were asked to rate six theoretical frameworks in regard to their usefulness in family therapy: psychodynamic, behavioral, learning, small groups, family theory, and existential. The responses suggested two equally ascendant theoretical frameworks: the psychodynamic, with its focus on beliefs about the personality dynamics of the family members; and the family theory system, with its focus on multipersonal systems dynamics. Interestingly, these two frameworks seem to correspond with the "analyst" and the "systems purist" dichotomy used by Beels and Ferber to describe the practice of their reactor group of family therapists.

While the GAP report (1970) recognized the epistemological and ideological differences inherent in these two dominant theoretical positions, it also predicted an eventual process of model building that would lead to an integrated view of family therapy involving the blending of these two positions. Indeed, to develop a view of the practice of family therapy reflected in their data, the authors constructed a hypothetical continuum portraying the range of family therapy belief and action systems. Three distinct but continuous theoretical orientations were proposed. At one extreme, position A, were those therapists who saw the family as a means of gathering information about specific family members. These therapists retained a primary focus on the individual and were contrasted with their hypothetical opposite, the position-Z therapists, who focused entirely on the family as the unit of both change and pathology. Consequently, position-Z therapists were more likely to view traditional psychiatric problems as social and interpersonal symptoms of maladaptive family functioning. Position-M therapists were conceptualized as eclectic middle-of-the-roaders who "saw equal validity in an approach to the individual and to the family system, and who might elect to use either or both system levels in conceptualizing about as well as in treating illness" (p. 48).

From the premises grounded in each of the three positions, the GAP report (1970) projected hypothetical therapeutic action systems for positions A, M, and Z, in regard to seven dimensions of therapeutic practice:

1. Whether the therapists saw family therapy as an additional method (treatment procedure) or whether it was viewed as a new conceptual orientation to treatment
2. Whether the identified patient was the focus of treatment or not
3. The relative importance of history (temporal orientation)
4. The use of diagnostic procedures
5. The therapist's role in the diagnostic process
6. The interpretation of affect
7. The operational procedures of the therapy

A comparison of the two extreme positions of the proposed continuum of theoretical orientation (positions A and Z) in regard to each of these treatment dimensions is summarized in Table 2–2.

Following the report of the GAP, the next attempt to classify and summarize the diversity within the field was reported by Vincent Foley in *An Introduction to Family Therapy* (1974), perhaps the first textbook on family therapy prepared primarily for university students. In search of "seminal family theorists" to represent the field, Foley interviewed the five "most influential" theorists, as identified in the GAP survey and by his own research (Foley, 1971). The five were Satir, Ackerman, Jackson, Haley, and Bowen. Foley compared the beliefs about family therapy espoused by each by profiling them in regard to three "critical issues": What is a family? What should the outcome of family therapy be? and How does the family change? Through the examination of written materials, personal correspondence, and personal interviews,

TABLE 2-2   The Group for the Advancement of Psychiatry's A–Z Typology of Family Therapy Practice.

Practice Dimensions	Position A	Position Z
Emphasis on method vs orientation	Method	Orientation
Identification of patient	Individual	Family
Importance of history	Very important	Not important
Diagnostic procedures	Formal, emphasized	Informal, de-emphasized
Therapist's role in diagnosis	Therapist excluded	Therapist included
Affect	Family affective responses encouraged and interpreted	Affective responses de-emphasized
Operational procedures	Formal, delineated	Informal, flexible

Source: Group for the Advancement of Psychiatry. *Treatment of Families in Conflict.* New York: Science House, 1970.

he also scrutinized therapeutic action systems by summarizing the relative emphasis each gave to eight dimensions of the therapeutic role: history, diagnosis, affect, learning, values, conscious versus unconscious, transference, and therapist as teacher.

The responses to the "critical issues" (belief systems) questions posed by Foley are summarized in Table 2–3. Two patterns seem particularly prominent from the table. The first illustrates the internal consistency in regard to belief systems in each of the models. The definitions of a family utilized by the seminal theorists consistently circumscribe the targeted outcomes and imply model-specific processes for achieving them. The second pattern suggests a goodness of fit among the seminal theorists with the GAP's proposed A to Z continuum (GAP, 1970). Ackerman clearly reflected position A (psychodynamic). He was reluctant to describe the family as a system, viewing it as the primary unit for the socialization of personalities. The desired outcomes reflected attention to individual family members, and the prescription for change was described in terms of the modification of individual personalities. While each of the remaining four theorists described the family as a system and the general relevance of interpersonal dynamics with regard to both the outcome and nature of change, it is clear that systems-level thinking is applied more consistently across each of the three questions for Jackson and Haley than for Bowen and Satir. The latter two theorists qualify as position-M therapists, meshing individual and systems-level responses to the

TABLE 2-3　Foley's Comparison of the Belief Systems of Seminal Theorists.

| Theorists | What Is a Family? | Critical Issues | |
		Family Therapy Outcome	How Families Change
Ackerman	Group of interlocking personalities	Dissolving conflict; promoting positive personalities	Corrective, emotional experiences; insight
Bowen	System	Differentiation of self	Define self in relation to system
Haley	System	Disruption of existing interactional patterns	Re-establish appropriate power relationships
Jackson	System	Recognition of rules; development of new rules	System disequilibriation
Satir	System	Understanding of self	Learning new communication patterns

Source: V. D. Foley. *An Introduction to Family Therapy.* New York: Grune and Stratton, 1974.

questions posed. While Bowen views the family as an emotional system, both the therapeutic goals and the process of change are connected to greater levels of individual differentiation of family members from the family system. Similarly, Satir focuses on such family systems concepts as rules while at the same time connecting the change process and the desired outcome to increasing levels of self-understanding. On the other hand, Jackson and Haley, the position-Z therapists, maintain the interpersonal focus in regard to both therapeutic outcome and the process of change.

Table 2–4 summarizes Foley's analysis (1974) of the eight dimensions of therapeutic action on which he compared the influential therapists with regard to convergence and divergence. Each was evaluated and assigned the value of high (H), medium (M), or low (L) with regard to the emphasis placed on that dimension by the theorist. As can be seen from the table, the five theorists converged on two dimensions (learning and therapist as model/teacher), suggesting that each of the theorists sees therapy as a learning process either facilitated

TABLE 2-4 Foley's Comparison of Seminal Theorists' Action Systems.

						Dimensions		
Theorist	History	Diagnosis	Affect	Learning	Values	Conscious vs. Unconscious	Transference	Model/Teacher
N. Ackerman	M	H	H	H	H	M	M	H
M. Bowen	H	M	L	H	H	M	L	H
D. Jackson	M	M	L	H	H	M	L	H
J. Haley	L	L	M	H	M	L	L	H
V. Satir	H	L	H	H	M	L	L	H

Key: H = High; dimension emphasized
M = Medium; dimension considered but not of primary importance
L = Low; dimension de-emphasized
Source: V. D. Foley. *An Introduction to Family Therapy.* New York: Grune and Stratton, 1974.

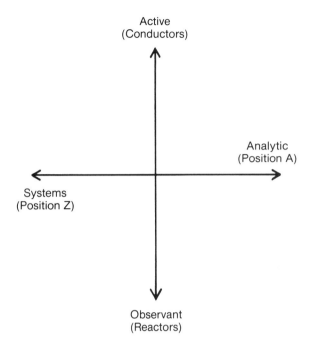

FIGURE 2-1 Foley's View of Family Therapy Belief and Action Systems (1974) Reconciled with Beels and Ferber (1969) and with the GAP Report (1970).

(Satir) or directed (Haley) by the therapist. On the other hand, the five theorists radically diverge in regard to the dimensions of history, diagnosis, and affect, while differing moderately for the dimensions of values, the importance of unconscious processes, and transference.

Unfortunately Foley was not able to complete his data collection plan for each of the theorists as he had intended. In addition, the degree to which the practice of these influential theorists was being replicated by practitioners oriented to their respective approaches is not addressed. Nevertheless, in an attempt to generalize from his comparisons of these significant pioneers in the field of family therapy, Foley essentially reaffirmed the polar distribution of action systems suggested in 1969 by Beels and Ferber (conductors versus reactors), as well as the belief system continuum suggested in 1970 by the GAP report (systems versus analytic). His two-dimensional diagrammatic representation of the field is depicted in Figure 2–1. Foley stopped short of attempting to place these influential therapists and their adherents on both of these axes and, more important, did not suggest whether particular belief and action systems characteristic of the field tended to covary or whether they may be adhered to independently of one another.

This question, however, was addressed by Philip Guerin (1976), who surveyed the family field and noted a conceptual shift among practitioners away from the A or psychodynamic position and toward the Z or systems-oriented position. He attributed this shift to increased efforts on the part of systems-oriented practitioners to articulate their positions as well as to the death of Ackerman and the subsequent decline of his influence on the growth of the field. Dissatisfied with the emphasis of previous attempts to describe the field with regard to variation in therapeutic style and the therapist's personality, Guerin suggested that well-defined theories or sets of belief systems about family therapy were subject to a number of varying stylistic in-terpretations. His schema reflected the growing view within the field that the A-to-Z typology did not reflect a continuum but rather repre-sented two dichotomous and mutually exclusive camps (Armstrong, 1972; Haley, 1968).

More sensitive to conceptual variation among the systems-oriented schools, perhaps because of his own position as an "insider" within this group, Guerin divided the analytic therapists into four categories: individual, group, experiential, and "Ackerman-type." The *individual* category was composed of those therapists who saw families "only when it was necessary to deal with situations in which a member or members of the family of the individual patient were undoing the process that was taking place in individual therapies" (Guerin, 1976, p. 18). The *group* category was formed by analytically oriented therapists who treated the family using principles of analytic group therapy. Citing Lyman Wynne and Chris Beels as representatives of this school, Guerin defined the therapeutic role as an observational one in which the therapist acted only to direct or clarify group process or to make dynamic interpretations. Guerin traced the origin of the analytically oriented *experiential* therapists to the human potential movement of the late 1960s. These practitioners tended to value and consequently guide the family toward discussions of their experience within the time and space of the therapy session. While recognizing the changing nature of the former's orientation, Guerin cited Carl Whitaker and Andrew Ferber as early proponents of this position. The final analytic category, the *Ackermanian,* was described as a nonreproducible method of in-tervention. Since it was seen as so strongly tied to Ackerman's per-sonality, and since Ackerman was reluctant to give up his orientation

TABLE 2-5 Guerin's Classification of the Systems–Oriented Family Therapies.

Therapy	Focus	Philosophy	View of Education
Bowenian	Growth	Idealistic; free-will	Explicit; cognitive
Strategic	Symptom	Pessimistic; deterministic	Implicit; experiential
Structural	Symptom	Pessimistic; deterministic	Implicit; experiential

Source: P. J. Guerin. *Family Therapy: Theory and Practice.* New York: Gardner Press, 1976.

as an analyst, Guerin argued that a clearly delineated family theory never emerged from his work.

To profile the growing differentiation among the systems-oriented therapists, Guerin (1976) identified three parameters on which these approaches could be compared: the therapeutic focus (symptom or growth), the degree of optimism about the malleability of human behavior, and the type of education emphasized. He listed four systems approaches to family therapy: the structural, the strategic, the Bowenian, and the general systems. This latter group was not classified in regard to Guerin's threefold scheme because he saw it as being concerned with "the larger social context both in order to understand behavior and to mobilize forces to alter the context" (p. 20). Since Guerin observed that the thinking representing this approach had not been operationalized as a family therapy, he did not clarify it with regard to his identified dimensions. While previous attempts to describe the family therapy field have included the approaches of both Bowen and Haley, Guerin's effort recognized the national prominence achieved in the 1970s by Minuchin and his structural approach.

Guerin's typology, summarized in Table 2–5, clearly emphasizes the similarity between Minuchin's structural approach and Haley's strategic approach. The compatibility of these two approaches at this point reflects the six-year period of collaboration of the two at the Philadelphia Child Guidance Center (1967–1973). Guerin's typology also illuminates the joint departure of these two approaches from the Bowenian perspective on all three dimensions.

Sharing Guerin's concern with the importance of theory in the overall knowledge expansion and verification process, Ritterman

(1977) examined the differences between Minuchin's structural approach and the communications-oriented approach that had evolved from the work of the Mental Research Institute (MRI) investigations. Arguing that a philosophical world view or "pre-theoretical assumptions" shape both theory and practice, Ritterman distinguished between these two approaches to family therapy by linking them to historically different and mutually exclusive ways of ordering natural and social phenomena. The communications approach was placed within the context of the Newtonian–Gallilean or mechanistic world view. Ritterman argued that this philosophical commitment is guided by the belief in "elementalism," or the search for fundamental or irreduceable elements of social wholes (e.g., essential "bits" of intrafamily communication, or message units). Congruent with this overriding and orienting belief, family pathology is assumed to be the result of linear events (antecedent–consequent causality) in which message X may be observed to cause message Y and/or behavior Z. Consequently, the treatment focus is toward the removal of identified symptoms by identifying and modifying or eliminating these causal sequences.

Ritterman (1977) placed Minuchin's structural approach within the context of the alternative organismic world view. With its origins in biology, this perspective emphasizes the organization of phenomena by attending to "wholism," or the belief that the whole is greater than the sum of its parts. It is characterized by a belief in reciprocal causality that "provides for a dialectical analysis of the relationship between part-processes in what is called the organized complexity of the whole" (p. 31). Consequently, structural family therapy is less concerned with the particular sequences of communicational acts and the removal of symptoms. Rather, it attempts to restructure the family system by attending to the basic properties of family organization that govern the transactions of its members.

While Ritterman's schema, like Guerin's, served to highlight differences in theory rather than therapeutic style, it by and large has not been useful to the field. It clearly implied a value judgment, as both Weakland (1977) and Levant (1980) have since pointed out, by aligning one school (the structural) with a more recent and presumably more valid philosophical world view. As Weakland (1977) described Ritterman's schema, "Good things like spontaneity and open systems are related to the 'organismic view,' and bad ones like materialism and closed systems to the mechanistic view—as if the term mechanistic did not already have a negative enough connotation" (p. 47). In addition, Ritterman did not attempt to place the full range of family therapies on the elementaristic–wholistic dimension. Consequently, she did not face squarely the issue of the placement of such theorists as Haley, who has been instrumental in the development of both the structural and the communications approaches, and Carl Whitaker, whom she acknowledges cannot be placed.

The final attempt to classify the family therapies in the 1970s was made by Madanes and Haley (1977), who developed a practical schema for organizing and comparing the therapies in the field. To do so they identified seven "dimensions which characterize most therapy" (p. 89) and reflect both belief and action systems. These dimensions were:

1. The temporal orientation or relative emphasis given to the family's past or present
2. The use of interpretation and whether interpretation is used to unravel the past or the present
3. Whether the goals are linked to growth or the presenting problem
4. Whether the therapy procedure is characterized by the application of a method or whether problem-specific plans are developed on a case-by-case basis
5. The unit of treatment (whether 1, 2, or 3 persons are involved)
6. Whether family hierarchies or egalitarianism are attended to
7. Whether human behavior is viewed digitally (with reference to observable events) or analogically (with reference to the meaning of events in the context of other events)

Like the GAP report (1970) and Guerin (1976), Madanes and Haley (1977) observed two categories of family therapy: those therapies that represent an *adaptation* of individual thought to family therapy (the psychodynamic, the experiential, and the behavioral) and those that have *evolved* with the family therapy movement (the extended family, the structural, and the strategic). The latter three approaches correspond to Guerin's (1976) description of the systems therapies, except that Guerin's Bowenian typology has been expanded to include the social network therapy of Speck and Attneave (1973), the family of origin therapy of Framo (1976), and the generational therapy of Boszormenyi-Nagy and Spark (1973).

Table 2–6 summarizes Madanes and Haley's (1977) description of the family therapy movement with regard to characteristics that comprise each of these seven major dimensions. Their work suggests patterns of both convergence and divergence within and across the approaches comprising the "evolved" and the "adapted" categories of

TABLE 2-6 Madanes and Haley's Comparison of Approaches to Family Therapy by Characteristics Comprising Seven Dimensions of Theory and Therapy.

Characteristic of Dimension	"Adapted" Approaches			"Evolved" Approaches		
	Psychodynamic	Experiential	Behavioral	Structural	Strategic	Extended Family
Past	+	+	0	0	0	0
Interpret (past)	+	+	0	0	0	0
Present	0	+	+	+	+	+
Interpret (present)	+	+	0	+	0	+
1-person-unit	+	+	+	0	0	0
2-person-unit	0	0	+	+	+	+
3-person-unit	0	0	0	+	+	+
Method	+	+	0	0	0	+
Growth	+	+	0	+	0	+
Analogical	+	+	0	+	+	+
New experience	0	+	+	+	+	0
Directives	0	0	+	+	+	+
Plan for therapy	0	0	+	+	+	0
Hierarchy	0	0	0	+	+	+
Presenting problem	0	0	+	0	+	0
Digital	0	0	+	0	+	0

Key: + = the presence or emphasis of a characteristic
0 = the absence or de-emphasis of a characteristic

Source: Adapted from C. Madanes & J. Haley, Dimensions of Family Therapy. Journal of Nervous and Mental Disease, 165, 1977, 88–97.

family therapy. With regard to convergence among the "evolved" approaches (the extended family, the structural, and the strategic), three dimensions are shared. Each approach emphasizes the present as opposed to the past in therapy, each advocates the treatment of a relationship unit comprised of two or three people, and each emphasizes the hierarchical nature of family relationships. Interestingly, although Madanes and Haley highlighted the shared nature of the development of the strategic and structural schools, the extended family and structural approaches emerged as the most similar among the systems therapies. They differed only in regard to one dimension of therapy, the method/plan category. The extended family approach was characterized by the application of standard procedures and techniques across all cases, while Madanes and Haley typified the structural and strategic approach as advocating specific plans for each family/ problem. The structural and strategic approaches converged on four dimensions (temporal orientation, specific plan for each case, treating two- and three-person problems, and emphasizing the hierarchical nature of family relations), and the extended family and strategic converged on three (temporal orientation, the problem unit, and emphasis on family hierarchies).

In regard to the similarities between each of these systems approaches and the three approaches with origins in individual therapy, the strategic approach converged with the behavioral approach on four dimensions (temporal orientation, interpretation, the treatment of presenting problems, and the use of treatment plans rather than the application of a method). A less clear pattern of convergence was noted for the structural approach, which converged with each of the three "adapted" approaches on two dimensions; and for the extended family approach, which converged with the psychodynamic and experiential approaches on three dimensions each.

The 1980s: Toward Larger Constructs

As the family therapy enterprise occupies its third decade, efforts to portray the similarities and differences among approaches to family therapy practice have attended to both the action systems emphasized in the typologies of the 1960s as well as the belief systems that became paramount to the classification attempts of the 1970s. A discernible shift in the family therapy literature also can be observed, however, from a review of the efforts to typify the family therapy movement in the 1980s. As Olson, Russell, and Sprenkle (1980) noted in a decade review of the literature, there has been a declining influence of singular family therapy exemplars and pioneers in the provision of benchmarks for referencing theoretical orientations in the field. Consequently, while the divergence emphasized during the decades of the 1960s and 1970s continues to organize thematically some of the classification schemes of the 1980s (Horne and Ohlsen, 1982; Jones, 1980), other efforts have attempted to locate common threads among the family therapies. These latter efforts have proceeded without an exclusive and perhaps confining focus on either belief or action system. Rather, they have built upon and perhaps moved beyond the unidimensional foci of the 1960s on action systems and the 1970s on belief systems, through two somewhat similar methods of classification. The first method is characterized by the merging of two or more "unique" approaches into more inclusive "schools" or models (Gurman & Kniskern, 1981; Hansen & L'Abate, 1982; Hoffman, 1981; Olson et al., 1980), while the second focuses more on the identification, merging, or collapsing of significant themes, concepts, or larger constructs with less attention to identifiable schools or models of family therapy (L'Abate & Frey, 1981; Levant, 1980).

The first major attempt to classify the field in the 1980s extended the work of the 1970s by attending to the variation in belief systems among several family therapy approaches. Susan Jones' *Family Therapy: A Comparison of Approaches* (1980) describes seven approaches to family therapy along with the developers/exemplars of each:

1. Integrative (Ackerman)
2. Psychoanalytic (Framo, Steirlin, and Grotjahn)
3. Bowenian (Bowen)
4. Structural (Minuchin)
5. Interactional (Jackson, Watzlawick, Haley, and Satir)
6. Social network (Speck, Attneave, and Rueveni)
7. Behavioral (Patterson)

Jones analyzes each in regard to four major areas: the therapeutic unit, the major concepts, the goal of treatment, and the treatment process itself.

In Table 2–7, the seven approaches are compared with one another in regard to beliefs about family behavior and the therapeutic process, focusing on the type of system emphasized, whether pathology is viewed internally (personality dynamics) or externally (personal relations), and the manner in which breakdown in family functioning is defined. As the table suggests, variation among these seven ap-

TABLE 2-7 Jones' Comparison of the Belief Systems of Seven Family Therapy Approaches.

Therapy	Family as a System	Locus of Pathology	Breakdown in Family Functioning
Integrative	No	Equal weight to internal and external	Fluidity or rigidity of family role relationships
Psychoanalytic	Psychological system	Emphasize internal	Introjection of parental figures
Structural	Transactional structural system	Emphasize external	Enmeshed or disengaged family boundaries
Interactional	Behavioral-communication system	Emphasize external	Ambiguity of family rules that define the family relationship
Bowen	Emotion and relationship system	Emphasize internal	Introjection of parental figures
Social Network	?	Emphasize external	Loss of resilience in family social network
Behavioral	Interlocking behavioral system	External only	Maladaptive learning

Source: S. Jones: *Family Therapy: A Comparison of Approaches.* Bowie, MD.: Robert J. Brady Co., 1980.

proaches is portrayed primarily in regard to the type of system the family is thought to reflect or emphasize and in regard to the indicators of breakdown. In regard to the locus of pathology (using the GAP's [1970] A, M, and Z positions), Jones clearly sees the majority of approaches (5) clustering either at the M position (emphasizing both internal and external dynamics) or at the Z position (emphasizing external dynamics exclusively). Only the psychoanalytic and the Bowenian approaches fall within the GAP's A position, through an emphasis on an internal locus of pathology.

To compare the seven selected approaches with regard to the prescribed therapeutic process, Jones examined the composition of the patient or treatment unit, the importance of history, the importance of insight, and whether or not the therapist joins in or attempts to become

TABLE 2-8 Jones' Comparison of the Therapeutic Processes of Seven Family Therapy Approaches.

Therapy	Who Is the patient?	Is History Important?	Is Insight Necessary?	Does the Therapist Join the System?
Integrative	Individual and family	Yes	Yes	Yes, via a transference relationship
Psychoanalytic	Individual and family	Yes	Yes	Yes, via a transference relationship
Structural	Family only	No	No	Yes, to form a therapeutic system
Interactional	Family only	No	No	Yes, to form a therapeutic system
Bowen	Individual and family	Yes	Yes	No, must not be triangled into system
Social network	Family only	No	No	Yes, to become part of the social network
Behavioral	Individual and family	No	No	Yes, to role model for family

Source: S. Jones: *Family Therapy: A Comparison of Approaches.* Bowie, MD.: Robert J. Brady Co., 1980.

an interactional part of the family unit. Table 2–8 summarizes Jones' schema of the seven approaches in regard to each of these four therapeutic process dimensions.

Viewed within Jones' context, clear patterns of both convergence and divergence among the seven approaches emerge in regard to views about the enactment of the therapeutic role. In regard to convergence, two strikingly similar pairs of approaches are evidenced. The integrative and psychoanalytic and the structural and the interactional are congruent across each of the four dimensions of therapeutic process. With regard to divergence, the dimensions of history and insight appear to be particularly important. These dimensions discriminate the two pairs of approaches from one another as well as create additional cleavages across all seven of the approaches. Family history is important to three of the approaches and unimportant to four, while insight is a necessary condition for change from the perspective of the same three approaches and unnecessary from the perspective of the remaining four.

Alan Gurman and David Kniskern organize their landmark *Handbook of Family Therapy* (1981) through merging several schools of family therapy. In what may prove to be one of the most enduring volumes of the decade, the editors brought together comprehensive descriptions of the work of 15 recognized leaders in the field. These descriptions were prepared by the family therapists themselves and were in response to a twelvefold format devised by the editors:

1. Detailed description of the background of the approach
2. The view of family health
3. The view of family pathology
4. The assessment of system dysfunction
5. Goal setting in therapy
6. Treatment applicability
7. The structure of the therapy process
8. The role of the therapist
9. Techniques of treatment
10. Curative factors in the treatment approach
11. The effectiveness of the approach
12. The training of therapists

Unfortunately, the editors make no attempt to provide a systematic comparison of the 15 approaches utilizing this extensive analytic framework. To their credit, however, Gurman and Kniskern do order these approaches by identifying and placing each within one of four major schools of family therapy: the psychoanalytic and object relations approaches, the intergenerational approaches, the systems theory approaches, and the behavioral approaches. Table 2–9 lists each of these schools and the constituent family therapies that comprise them.

Hansen and L'Abate (1982) utilize a historical approach in their ordering of the field. In a manner similar to that of Madanes and Haley, they suggest that some schools of family therapy represent historical adaptations or mutations of the three organizing foci for individual therapy: the humanistic, the psychodynamic, and the behavioral. To complete their typology they add a fourth group, the "systems," which they describe as having no historical antecedent among the individual

TABLE 2-9 Gurman and Kniskern's View of the Family Therapy Field.

Major Models	Representative Approaches
Psychoanalytic and object relations	Group analytic couples therapy
Intergenerational	Family of origin Contextual Symbolic-experiential Bowenian
Systems	Interactional Structural Strategic Functional Problem-centered Integrative
Behavioral	Parent training Marital therapy Sexual dysfunction therapy

Source: A. S. Gurman & D. P. Kniskern (Eds.). *Handbook of Family Therapy*. New York: Brunner/Mazel, 1981.

models of therapy. Hansen and L'Abate's classification of the schools of family therapy using their historical frame of reference is summarized in Table 2–10.

In a third attempt to both array and collapse the schools of family therapy during the 1980s, Olson et al. (1980) sketched four major schools and described representative theories and theorists for each: the structural, the strategic, the experiential, and the social learning. Curiously, the Bowenian school was excluded, without explanation. Reflecting the authors' observation of the declining organizational influence of singular theorists, the strategic school was described with reference to three approaches: Haley's problem-solving method, the communicational approach of the MRI (Watzlawick, Beavin, & Jackson, 1967; Watzlawick, Weakland, & Fisch, 1974; Watzlawick & Weakland, 1977), and the systemic group approaches introduced by Selvini in Italy and advocated in the United States by Papp (1977, 1980) and Hoffman (1981).

The fourth and final effort to group the family therapies by overriding schools of thought provided the organization for Lynn Hoffman's book, *Foundations of Family Therapy* (1981). The purpose of Hoffman's work was to integrate theory and techniques of family therapy. To provide a foundation for that attempt, her view of the field included three groups into which the family movement might be placed. The

TABLE 2-10 Hansen and L'Abate's Ordering of the Field by Schools and Representative Theorists.

Humanistic	Psychoanalytic	Behavioral	Systems
T. Gordon	N. Ackerman	G. Patterson	P. Watzlawick
R. Levant	M. Bowen	R. Stuart	S. Minuchin
C. Whitaker	I. Boszormenyi-Nagy	J. Alexander	M. Selvini-Palazzoli
A. Napier	J. Framo	F. Thomas	J. Haley
V. Satir	H. Steirlin	R. Weiss	G. Zuk
R. and B. Duhl		W. Jacobson	H. Laqueur
L. Constantine		R. Liberman	R. McGregor
W. Kempler			

Source: J. C. Hansen & L. L'Abate. *Approaches to Family Therapy*. New York: Macmillan, 1982.

first group, which she dubbed the "great originals," denied classification. They represent significant pioneering figures (some of whom are deceased) whose contributions continue to influence large numbers of family therapists, yet who have not formed schools of family therapy. These originals include Virginia Satir, the late Nathan Ackerman, the late Don Jackson, the late Milton Erikson, and Carl Whitaker.

Hoffman viewed the second group as tangential to the family therapy movement as a whole. This group included those approaches, such as gestalt and behavioral, which have developed independent of the family movement per se. Like Madanes and Haley (1977), Hoffman argued that the efforts of these schools represented attempts to make family therapy applicable to notions about human behavior that apply to individuals. Hoffman's final grouping of approaches to family therapy represented what she viewed as the major competing approaches in the field. They included those schools she referenced as the historical, the ecological, the structural, the strategic, and the systemic. Each of these schools and the theorists comprising them are listed in Table 2–11.

The final two approaches to classification of family therapies in the 1980s differed from those previously considered. While those already discussed either arrayed or merged available models, the final two approaches have built upon these typologies as well as those of the 1960s and 1970s by attempting to isolate larger organizing constructs that may cut across both the previously identified "schools" as well as their belief and action systems. The first of these attempts was reported by Ronald Levant (1980). As he surveyed previously developed schemata he observed that none seemed to include the range of available

TABLE 2-11 Hoffman's View of the Major Family Therapy Approaches and the Major Theorists Associated with Each.

Approach	Theorists
Historical	M. Bowen
	I. Boszormenyi-Nagy
	N. Paul
	H. Steirlin
Ecological	E. Augerswald
Structural	S. Minuchin
Strategic	J. Haley & C. Madaness
	J. Weakland & P. Watzlawick
Systematic	M. Selvini-Palazzoli

Source: L. Hoffman. *Foundation of Family Therapy*. New York: Basic Books, 1981.

family therapy approaches. He attributed this incompleteness to the deductive imposition of existing categories, arguing that knowledge in the field had grown from empirical observations made by researchers and clinicians in a wide variety of observational and treatment contexts. Consequently, to determine if the various models of family therapy cluster into conceptually distinguishable groups he began by aggregating and arraying the range of available family therapy concepts and subjected them to a method he described as a "qualitative factor analysis."

Levant's work (1980) produced one first- and one second-order factor. The first-order factor, *temporal orientation*, grouped the family therapies in regard to whether the focus of the therapy primarily emphasizes the past or the present. The second-order factor further distinguished among the present-oriented or ahistorical groups by reflecting two different perspectives with regard to desired therapeutic outcome. It dichotomized between those therapeutic endeavors that target either the family structure or process as the locus of change and those that primarily emphasize the provision of an intense affective experience for the family members. Levant referred to each of the three groups of family therapy approaches as paradigms: the historical, the structure/process, and the experiential.

The historical paradigm reflected cumulative observations suggested by previous typologies of the family therapy movement in the 1970s (Foley, 1974; Madanes & Haley, 1977) and in the 1980s (Gurman & Kniskern, 1981; Hoffman, 1981; Jones, 1980). It was distinguished by its concern with the resolution of historical ties or emotional attachments to the family of origin. The therapist's role is one of eliciting and using knowledge of family history, interpretation of behavior, coaching in regard to family interaction, and facilitating insight and the uncovering of unknown motivating factors. Levant viewed this paradigm as represented by three schools: the multigenerational (Bowen), the intergenerational (Nagy and Spark), and the psychodynamic (Wynne, Lidz, Framo, and Paul). It represented a commitment to psychodynamic theory, although, particularly in the instance of Bowen, that commitment may be more implicit than explicit.

Levant's structure/process paradigm (1980) represented the largest number of schools of family therapy; indeed, it included four of the five schools specified by Hoffman (1981) and three of the six profiled by Madanes and Haley (1977). Levant referenced the structure/process paradigm to include the communications (Jackson, Haley, Watzlawick, and Weakland), problem-solving (Haley), brief problem-focused (Watzlawick, Weakland, and Fisch), triadic (Zuk), structural (Minuchin), and behavioral (Patterson) schools, as well as the work of Virginia Satir, Selvini-Pallazzoli, Lynn Hoffman, and Peggy Papp. While some of the constituent therapies attend to family structure (Minuchin) and other processes (Satir), Levant (1980) found common ground in the prevailing therapeutic goal of reordering or rearranging family systems to eliminate dysfunctional aspects of interaction that produce or maintain particular symptoms. The therapeutic role was concerned less with the psychology of the family members and more with the facilitation of systematic problem solving and planned, directive intervention.

Levant's final paradigm (1980), the experiential, is constituted by those schools of therapy that, by and large, define the outcome of the therapeutic process as one of personal growth for family members. This paradigm includes the gestalt approach (Kempler), the experiential (Whitaker, Malone, Napier, and Ferber), and the client-centered (Van DerVeen). The overall therapeutic goal is a provision of an intense affective experience among and between family members, which the therapist facilitates by joining the family, reflecting his understanding of family process, and modeling genuineness and reciprocity.

The second attempt of the 1980s to classify the family therapies across models and schools was completed by L'Abate and Frey (1981). The procedures utilized, however, differed from those followed by Levant. While Levant began with an inventory of family therapy concepts and developed his paradigms inductively, L'Abate and Frey began with core belief systems that typify all therapeutic methodologies and worked deductively to apply them to the range of family therapies.

L'Abate and Frey (1981) suggest that psychologies of the self as well as metapsychologies of human systems tended to emphasize, prioritize, or explain one of the three domains of human existence—emotionality, rationality, or activity (ERA)—while optional human functioning is contingent upon the balance of all three. They detect a waning emphasis upon an understanding of the role of emotionality or affect within the family therapy movement and consequently argue for their inclusive ERA model, which gives equal weight to emotionality (E, affect), rationality, (R, cognition), and activity (A, behavior).

The application of the ERA model to the family field is summarized in Table 2–12. Interestingly, the resultant clustering of schools and approaches is strikingly consistent with Levant's (1980) inductively constructed paradigms. The E school, represented by Satir, Napier, and Whitaker, is consonant with Levant's experiential paradigm. L'Abate and Frey (1981), like Levant, describe these therapies as prioritizing how feelings are experienced, expressed, and interpreted within family transactions. While Levant categorized the work of Satir within his structure/process paradigm, an examination of her work and the eclecticism it represents (Gurman, 1978) suggests her humanistic communications therapy would be equally if not more at home within the present emotionality category.

The R or rationality school is represented by the work of Boszormenyi-Nagy, Sparks, Steirlin, Bowen, and Framo. Again the categorization of these schools corresponds with the historical paradigm of Levant. The R school is distinguished by its psychoanalytic and cognitive prioritization of the role of thinking in overall family and individual functioning.

TABLE 2–12 L'Abate and Frey's ERA System of Classification of Family Therapy Theories.

Emotionality (E)	Rationality (R)	Activity (A)
V. Satir	I. Boszormenyi-Nagy	Adlerians
R. Bandler and J. Grinder	H. Steirlin	Palo Alto Group
A. Napier	M. Bowen	Milan Group
C. Whitaker	J. Framo	Behaviorism
.		S. Minuchin
		J. Haley

Source: L. L'Abate & J. Frey. The ERA model: The role of feelings in family therapy reconsidered: Implications for a classification of theories of family therapy. *Journal of Marital and Family therapy*, 1981, 7, 143–150.

Finally, the A or activity-oriented schools correspond to Levant's (1980) structure/process paradigm. The representative theorists suggested by L'Abate and Frey (1981), while as comprehensive as the list suggested by Levant (1980), are systems and/or behaviorally oriented and all emphasize "actual change outside of the office therapy by prescribed rituals, changes in relationships, and dual schedules" (L'Abate & Frey, 1981, p. 148).

Summary and Conclusions

To place our study in a historical perspective, in this chapter we have traced the cumulative conceptual efforts to profile the branching and segmentation that has accompanied the unprecedented growth of the family therapy movement. Our review of the literature has suggested that, like previous classification systems of individual psychotherapy, efforts to profile the convergence and divergence among the various approaches to family therapy have focused on two dimensions of theoretical orientation: (1) what practitioners believe to be true about human behavior and the process of therapy (belief systems) and (2) what they actually do in therapy (action systems).

Because theory was being developed almost exclusively in reaction to clinical practice in the early years, the first efforts in the 1960s to enumerate and compare the family therapies focused primarily on therapeutic action systems. They tended to be primarily descriptive and accentuated the varying therapeutic styles of the more prominent figures in the field. These early attempts emphasized the variation in personality among the pioneering practitioners and suggested that theoretical orientation to a given model of family therapy might be influenced strongly by the therapists' personal makeup.

The efforts to classify the family therapies in the 1970s continued to focus on the practice of the founders of the movement and of the subsequently established exemplars in the field. Reflecting the efforts of the leading proponents of family therapy to state and clarify their approaches to practice with families, however, the typologies that were developed attended to both belief and action systems and produced a number of specific dimensions of family therapy practice on which similarities and differences might be observed.

Finally, our review suggests that the work of the 1980s, while obviously not yet near completion, is much more difficult to summarize. On the one hand we did observe a continuation of the efforts of the mid-to-late 1970s to array and emphasize conceptual differences between the rapidly proliferating number of family therapies. On the other hand, however, we also observed an opposite trend, more compatible with efforts of the early 1970s, to collapse several schools or merge concepts and thereby suggest a fewer number of conceptually different approaches to the practice of family therapy.

In 1960 Murray Bowen used the analogy of six blind men and an elephant to describe the then-embryonic field of family therapy (Bowen, 1975). Each blind man felt a different part of the elephant and rendered a different description, based on the anatomical part to which he attended. Collectively the diverse conclusions that our literature review has suggested about the nature and consequently the number of different family therapies may reflect an even more profound dilemma for the field today than Bowen described almost 25 years ago. Indeed, the conflicting typologies we have reviewed may have served more to generate confusion in the field than to provide the order and clarity upon which future professional growth must be based.

It is abundantly apparent, therefore, that this confusion with regard to what the field of family therapy "looks like" begs for an empirical test. Such a test would provide the field with a beginning inventory of both the shared and divergent systems of therapeutic belief and action that characterize its members. It is equally apparent, however, that the same confusion within the field makes the selection of models for such a test rather precarious.

It became clear as we began the project that we could not test the full range of available approaches. The number of these approaches and the dimensions on which they needed to be compared were too numerous. Once we had settled on the idea of utilizing a limited number of recognized approaches, however, the problems of representativeness and inclusiveness quite obviously had to be addressed. In order to achieve representativeness and inclusiveness, therefore, our approach to model selection has been guided by a recognition of the two major referencing processes identified in the literature: the historical process of identifying approaches by particularly influential persons who developed and nurtured them, and the more recently identified tendency to group or merge several of these approaches with regard to more general and overriding characteristics. Consequently the family therapy approaches we have selected for empirical analysis are three: Virginia Satir's communications approach, Murray Bowen's approach (Bowenian), and Jay Haley and Salvadore Minuchin's structural/strategic approach. With regard to the first referencing process, each of these approaches was developed by early leaders in the field whose names continue to be associated, if not synonymous, with the practice of that particular form of family therapy. Finally, and with regard to the more recent theoretical-orientation referencing process of grouping approaches by larger overriding characteristics, these approaches each represent one of the three inclusive family therapy groupings suggested recently by Levant (1980) and by L'Abate and Frey (1981) and reviewed earlier in this chapter.

References

Ackerman, N. Family psychotherapy today. *Family Process,* 1970, *9,* 122–125.

Armstrong, R. Two concepts: Systems and psychodynamics, paradigms in collision? In J. Brandt & C. Moynihan (Eds.), *Systems therapy.* Washington, D.C.: Groome Center, 1972.

Beels, C. C., & Ferber, A. Family therapy: A view. *Family Process,* 1969, *8,* 280–332.

Boszormenyi-Nagy, I., & Spark, G. *Invisible loyalties: Reciprocity in intergenerational family therapy.* New York: Harper and Row, 1973.

Bowen, M. Family therapy after twenty years. In D. X. Freedman & J. E. Dyrud (Eds.), *American handbook of psychiatry* (vol. 5). New York: Basic Books, 1975.

Foley, V. D. *An introduction to family therapy.* New York: Grune and Stratton, 1974.

Framo, J. L. Family of origin as a therapeutic resource for adults in marital and family therapy: You can and should go home again. *Family Process,* 1976, *15,* 193–210.

Group for the Advancement of Psychiatry. *Treatment of families in conflict.* New York: Science House, 1970.

Guerin, P. J. *Family therapy: Theory and practice.* New York: Gardner Press, 1976.

Gurman, A. S. Contemporary marital therapies: A critique and comparative analysis of psychodynamic, behavioral and systems theory approaches. In T. J. Paolino & B. S. McCrady (Eds.), *Marriage and marital therapy: Psychodynamic, behavioral and systems theory perspectives.* New York: Brunner/Mazel, 1978.

Gurman, A. S., & Kniskern, D. P. (Eds.). *Handbook of family therapy.* New York: Brunner/Mazel, 1981.

Haley, J. Whither family therapy. *Family Process,* 1962, *1,* 69–100.

Haley, J. Family experiments: A new type of experimentation. In D. Jackson (Ed.), *Communication, family and marriage.* Palo Alto, Calif.: Science and Behavior Books, 1968.

Hansen, J. C., & L'Abate, L. *Approaches to family therapy.* New York: Macmillan, 1982.

Hoffman, L. *Foundation of family therapy.* New York: Basic Books, 1981.

Horne, A. M., & Ohlsen, M. M. (Ed.). *Family counseling and therapy.* Itasca, Ill.: Peacock, 1982.

Jones, S. L. *Family therapy: A comparison of approaches.* Bowie, Md.: Brady, 1980.

L'Abate, L., & Frey, J. The e-r-a model: The role of feelings in family therapy reconsidered: Implications for a classification of theories of family therapy. *Journal of Marital and Family Therapy*, 1981, *7*, 143–150.

Levant, R. F. A classification of the field of family therapy: A review of prior attempts and a new paradigmatic model. *American Journal of Family Therapy*, 1980, *8*, 3–16.

Madanes, C., & Haley, J. Dimensions of family therapy. *Journal of Nervous and Mental Disease*, 1977, *165*, 88–97.

Olson, D. H., Russell, C. S., & Sprenkle, D. H. Marital and family therapy: A decade review. *Journal of Marriage and the Family*, 1980, *42*, 973–994.

Papp, P. (Ed.). *Family therapy: Full length case studies*. New York: Gardner Press, 1977.

Papp, P. The Greek chorus and other techniques of family therapy. *Family Process*, 1980, *19*, 45–58.

Ritterman, M. K. Paradigmatic classification of family therapy theories. *Family Process*, 1977, *16*, 29–48.

Speck, R. V., & Attneave, C. *Family networks*. New York: Random House, 1973.

Sundland, D. M. Theoretical orientations of psychotherapists. In A. Gurman & A. Razin (Eds.), *Effective psychotherapy*. New York: Pergamon Press, 1977.

Wallach, M. S., & Strupp, H. H. Dimensions of psychotherapists' activity. *Journal of Consulting Psychology*, 1964, *28*, 120–125.

Watzlawick, P. J., Beavin, J. H., & Jackson, D. D. *Pragmatics of human communication*. New York: W. W. Norton, 1967.

Watzlawick, P. J., & Weakland, J. (Eds.). *The interactional view*. New York: W. W. Norton, 1977.

Watzlawick, P. J., Weakland, J., & Fisch, R. *Change: Principles of problem formation and problem resolution*. New York: W. W. Norton, 1974.

Weakland, J. H. Comments on Ritterman's paper. *Family Process*, 1977, *16*, 46–48.

3

The National Scene

In the preceding chapters, we traced the evolution and segmentation in the knowledge base of family therapy over the last three decades through an identification and comparative analysis of the pioneers in the field and the key theoretical frameworks which undergirded each period. Such an approach, however, must be taken further; for, while the significant literature of the field that provides the data base for this approach is generated largely by a select group of pioneers of first- or second-wave generation family therapy theorists (Thaxton & L'Abate, 1982), the "ripple effects" of these waves upon practicing family therapists hardly can be predicted by the earlier writings of the field's pioneers. Similarly, the "goodness of fit" between what the pioneers of any particular family therapy model prescribe about the dynamics of the therapeutic process and how, in fact, that model actually performs within the therapeutic encounter can only be evaluated by an attempt to describe these transactions empirically. Indeed, in many ways it is this ripple effect, enacted by subsequent generations of family therapists, that forms the basis for predicting the evolution of the knowledge and practice base of family therapy.

In this and the chapter that follows, therefore, we will present data from two nationwide surveys of practicing family therapists who reflect varying degrees of adherence to three of the major models of family therapy: communications, structural/strategic, and Bowenian. In the present chapter, data secured from members of the American Association for Marriage and Family Therapy (AAMFT) and the American Family Therapy Association (AFTA) will be presented. In Chapter 4 we will present similar data from graduates of the major training programs/networks of the same three models of family therapy. Ultimately, in both chapters we will attempt to use the data bases derived from a significant pool of practicing family therapists to describe and compare these three models of family therapy empirically, thereby providing some opportunity for a "reality test" of the expanding knowledge base provided by the literature within the interdisciplinary profession of family therapy.

Methodology

In the winter of 1979, questionnaires were mailed to the almost 6500 members of either the American Association for Marriage and Family Therapy or the American Family Therapy Association. Data in five basic areas were secured from the respondents. The first area constituted the respondents' "belief system," and was comprised of 33 statements or assumptions about the processes and goals of family therapy. In response to this Family Therapist's Assumption Scale, the respondents indicated their degree of agreement or disagreement (using a six-point modified Likert scale) to such statements as "The therapist cannot avoid becoming an interacting member of the family system."

The second area pertained to the respondents' "action system," or their in-session behaviors, asking how descriptive each of 26 style items was of their own practice. Examples of items from this Family Therapist's In-session Style Inventory included "provoking" and "modeling."

While the first two variable sets utilized instrumentation that was developed by the authors, the third variable set used an established, standardized instrument to provide a profile of the respondents' personality attributes. The 16PF (Cattell & Eber, 1962) consists of 181 items measuring 16 personality factors operationalized into polar adjectives. While a number of standardized personality inventories with noteworthy reliability and validity estimates were available to us, the attributes represented on the 16PF provide particularly comprehensive coverage of significant personality variables identified in the family therapy literature. In particular, this instrument operationalizes both the attributes of therapists (e.g., outgoing versus reserved; experimenting versus conservative) and the client outcome attributes (self-sufficient versus group dependent) identified in Chapter 2.

The fourth set of variables provided background data about the respondents, including information profiling their prior and current professional experiences, as well as their current practice activities.

The fifth and final variable set assessed the respondents' strength of theoretical adherence or orientation to each of the three models of family therapy selected for this national survey of practitioners. This Theoretical Orientation Scale, in its original form, consisted of listings of nine publications and nine authors and asked the respondents to rate the degree to which each expressed ideas about the practice of family therapy that were congruent with their own theoretical framework. In addition, a third listing of nine concepts was included in this scale, asking the respondents to indicate the degree to which each concept guided their own practice. Three publications, three authors, and three concepts were selected to represent each of the three models of family therapy. As was the case for the assumption and style items, the items included in the Theoretical Orientation Scale also were selected from the writings of the exemplars of each of the three models of family therapy under investigation, so as to provide representative coverage of each.

Because of the obvious breadth of the data pool, the five variable sets just described were distributed in four overlapping questionnaire forms, which then were mailed randomly to the AAMFT and AFTA membership. The return rate for this national survey of AAMFT and AFTA membership was almost one-fourth (23.9%), after adjusting for incorrect mailing addresses, dual membership, and so forth. This return rate provided 1451 usable questionnaires.

A composite profiling of these 1451 respondents indicates that their averaged age was 42.8 years, with the youngest being 24 and the oldest 80, with a median age of 41 years. Over two-thirds (69.1%) of the respondents were male, with four-fifths (79.1%) having master's degrees and two-fifths (39.6%) having doctorates. Overall this was a very highly educated and experienced group of professional practitioners, as they averaged 9.5 years of practice in providing family therapy, 9.9 years in providing individual therapy, and 4.9 years in providing group therapy. Finally, they also were involved in a number of training-related activities, including an average of 4.4 years of experience as clinical supervisors, 3.1 years in staff development, and 2.8 years in university teaching.

Now let us take a closer look at the instrumentation. For all three of the scales we developed (the 33-item Family Therapist's Assumption Scale, the 26-item Family Therapist's In-session Style Inventory, and the 27-item Theoretical Orientation Scale), we performed additional data analyses to revise these scales before comparisons among the three models of family therapy were pursued.

Theoretical Orientation Scale

For the Theoretical Orientation Scale, we utilized a two-step scale construction process. First, individual-item-to-total-subscale-score correlations were generated for each of the three family therapy models represented in this scale. This item analysis procedure revealed that, for the communications and Bowenian models of family therapy, five of the nine items for each approach should be retained, including all three concepts, the exemplar (author) of that particular model (either Satir or Bowen), and a major publication of the respective exemplar. The range of item-to-total-score correlations for these remaining items was .65 to .72 (Pearson r) for the communications model's subscale, and .54 to .73 for the Bowenian model's subscale. For the structural/strategic model, seven of the nine items were retained, including the three concepts, the co-exemplars (Minuchin and Haley), and a major publication of each. Item-to-total-score correlations for these seven items ranged from .44 to .69.

In step two, computation of internal consistency (Cronbach's *Alpha*) for each of the revised subscales indicated an intercorrelation of .72 for the communications model's revised theoretical orientation subscale, .67 for the Bowenian model's five remaining items, and .73 for the structural/strategic model's seven remaining items. Appendix A portrays the items remaining for each of the three family therapy models' revised theoretical orientation subscales.

As a starting point, however, it is noteworthy that the average of all the scores of all respondents who completed the Theoretical Orientation Scale (N=1175) was 4.7 per item (on a six-point scale) for the five communications model items included in the revised Theoretical Orientation Scale, while it was only 3.78 for both the structural/strategic and Bowenian models' items. This higher "recognition" level for the communications model in this national sample may be surprising to some observers of the national family therapy scene, as the frequency of Virginia Satir's publications and the visibility and extent of her training endeavors do not appear to be demonstrably greater than those of the exemplars representing the two other models. Consequently, the reasons for the communications model's greater degree of popularity among the respondents to the national survey may be linked to the specific properties of the model itself. As we examine convergence and divergence among the three models, therefore, we pay particular attention to those belief and action systems that distinguish the communications model from the Bowenian and the structural/strategic models.

Family Therapist's Assumption Scale

The 33 items constituting the original Family Therapist's Assumption Scale were subjected to factor analysis employing varimax rotation and principle factoring with iteration. A factor-loading criterion of .30 was established, *a priori*. Twenty-one of the original 33 items loaded on one of the five factors. Table 3–1 lists the names as well as the constituent assumption items, with factor loadings for each of the assumption factors. The remaining 12 assumption items were eliminated from subsequent data analysis.

To examine the prevalence of the family therapy belief systems represented by each factor in our national sample of family therapists, an item mean for each respondent for each factor was calculated by dividing the sum of the scores for each item in a given factor by the total number of items in that factor. Thus, the range of factor scores for all of the assumption factors was between 1 and 6, regardless of the number of items included in a factor. We now will describe and discuss each of these factors, beginning with the factor receiving the highest endorsement on the six-point scale (Insight) and ending with the factor receiving the lowest item mean (Systemic View).

Insight. The item mean for the Insight factor for the 713 family therapists responding to the Family Therapist's Assumption Scale was 4.85. Indeed, the strength of the overall endorsement of this factor perhaps is reflected best in the fact that an overwhelming majority of the family therapists found these six items "descriptive" of their practice to some degree; for all six items, the item means on the six-point scale exceeded 3 for 95.3 percent of the responding therapists.

Inspecting these six items, we can see that the Insight factor prioritizes the use of communicational and interactional patterns among family members as a vehicle for enhancing self-awareness and achieving new understanding of the meaning of one's own, as well as significant others', behaviors. In addition, the items suggest that the release or expression of feelings and emotions provides the context for the development of this insight and, finally, that the family therapists' interpretation of behavior facilitates the achievement of these therapeutic goals.

Taken together, however, the six items that comprise this strongly endorsed factor are confounding when considered in the context of the

TABLE 3–1 Assumption Factors and Item Loadings: National Survey.

Factor	Factor Loadings
Factor I: Insight	
A family therapist should emphasize the feelings that family members have toward each other.	.68
A family therapist should share his/her perceptions of verbal and nonverbal behavior with family members in order to enable better understandings of the impact of their behavior.	.66
Change in family members' behaviors can be effected by helping each member to deal with his/her feelings about self and about the other family members.	.61
To be effective, the family therapist should provide alternative interpretations for family members' behaviors.	.51
By re-enacting or "mirroring" family members' patterns of relating, a family therapist can enable the family members to recognize their own behaviors and the impact of their behaviors on each other.	
Much of the process of family therapy focuses on the way in which family members send messages, the ways in which family members receive and interpret these messages, and the difficulties arising from a lack of understanding between sender and receiver.	.32
Factor II: Professional Growth	
Growth as an effective family therapist is dependent upon the pursuit of personal understanding and growth.	.59
To become an effective family therapist, one must actively explore and understand one's own position in one's family.	.59
The use of a cotherapist enhances the effectiveness of the conduct of family therapy.	.38
Appropriate self-disclosure by the therapist is a vital part of the conduct of family therapy.	.37
Factor III: Problem-Solving	
Change in family members' feelings about themselves and each other can be effected by showing them alternative patterns of behaving.	.49
Change in family members' behaviors can be effected by concentrating on the rational choices or options available.	.46

(continued)

TABLE 3-1 (continued)

Factor	Factor Loadings
Factor IV: A-traditionalism	
Change in a family system can be effected when working with only one member of the family.	.43
A therapist should take responsibility for directing the course of family therapy.	.36
Responsibility for the content and conduct of the family therapy session should be assumed by the family members.	−.33
A family therapist can facilitate change in the family by exaggerating the problem behavior.	.31
Factor V: Systemic View	
A family member can best effect change in his/her patterns of relating to present family members by effecting change in the patterns of relating to his/her family of origin.	.51
If a family member shares information with the family therapist, it should be shared with all members of the family.	.49
Regardless of the nature of the presenting problem, all members of the family should be involved on a continuing basis in family therapy.	.44
Behind every child's problem is a marital problem.	.37
Family therapy is not the appropriate model of intervention in all case situations.	−.37

family therapy literature reviewed in Chapter 2. While the endorsement of insight as a therapeutic goal has long characterized the nonbehavioral methods of individual counseling and psychotherapy, its pertinence and centrality within the therapeutic enterprise has been challenged by many family therapists. Indeed, as we have suggested earlier, historians of the family therapy movement repeatedly have credited the practitioner's disillusionment with the efficacy of insight in providing behavior change as instrumental to the development of family therapy practice in general and to the orientations of Jay Haley and Salvadore Minuchin in particular (Guerin, 1976; Jones, 1980). As further support for this we would cite our discussions of the "evolved" approaches portrayed in Table 2–6, as well as the structural, interactional, and behavioral approaches portrayed in Table 2–8.

Professional Growth.   The item mean for the four items comprising the Professional Growth factor was 4.69. Unlike the endorsement of the Insight factor, the high priority given this factor is quite congruent within the professional literature. Clearly, the cumulative emphasis on this factor rests upon the relationship between effective practice and the clinician's own growth as a professional. While we will discuss this relationship in greater depth in Chapter 6, we should note that the two highest-loaded items in this factor link clinical effectiveness to "personal understanding and growth," which may be facilitated through the exploration of the therapist's role and position within his/her family of origin. Essentially these items reflect a theme that cuts across many of the family therapies. While some therapy theories emphasize the therapist's growth within the emotional or feeling domain (Satir, 1972), others specify teaching/learning techniques that emphasize growth through development of more cognitively oriented areas (Kerr, 1981). At the same time we also should note that, once again, as with the Insight factor, this theme (Professional Growth) in fact plays a significantly less influential role for those approaches to family therapy described in Table 2–8 as structural, interactional, and behavioral.

The two additional items loading on the Professional Growth factor do so with lesser magnitudes. Clearly, the family therapy literature suggests that these items, respectively linking therapeutic effectiveness to the use of a cotherapist and to self-disclosure, represent more controversial practice issues. Bowen, for example, finds no utility in either technique. Indeed, his theoretical system suggests that the potential for triangulation of the therapist, inherent in both the use of a cotherapist and in the therapist's self-disclosure, makes these techniques antagonistic to positive therapeutic outcomes (Bowen, 1978; Kerr, 1981). On the other hand, Napier and Whitaker (1973) offer support for both, arguing that cotherapists in fact help to counteract the triangulation process and that self-disclosure is an essential element of the family therapist's spontaneity and creativity within the clinical process.

Problem Solving.   The factor that received the third highest item mean (4.25) was Problem Solving. While only two items comprised this factor, their uniform and central thrust seems to be on the importance of engaging the family in a problem-solving process. One item highlights the solving of problems through the therapist's provision of alternative problem-solving behaviors, while the second item emphasizes the therapist's role in shifting the process to a rational level or domain.

The relatively strong endorsement of this factor by the national sample of family therapists would appear to highlight a theme generic to the practice of family therapy. While we noted in Chapter 2 the strong allegiance of such pioneers as Minuchin and Haley to defining therapy as a problem-resolution enterprise, such theoreticians as Bowen and Satir also share components of this factor. Bowen stresses the therapist's role in shifting the therapeutic process and dialogue away from "emotional reactiveness" and toward cognitive problem understanding and solving, while Satir stresses the importance of moving beyond symptom resolution to help families learn new ways of coping with (and solving) existing as well as emerging problems. While perhaps we might draw a distinction between the first two exemplars' focus on the "problem" and the latter two exemplars' focus on the "solving" (process), what may join them together is this factor's emphasis on that which is observable and within the realm of one's conscious functioning, rather than on the unconscious or inaccessible aspects of behavior emphasized by more traditional, individual-oriented forms of therapy.

The meaning of the items comprising the Problem Solving factor should become more clear later, when we examine the relationship between our respondents' theoretical orientation and their responses on the Family Therapist's Assumption Scale.

A-traditionalism. The item mean for this factor (4.21) was similar to that observed for the Problem Solving factor. Comprised by four seemingly unrelated assumption items, this factor may suggest a belief system that is "a-traditional" or representative of clinical ideas that tend to go against the grain of traditional family therapy practice.

For example, the highest-loaded item in this factor states that "Change in a family system can be effected when working with only one member of the family." Although Bowen often advocates working with the most motivated members of the family, one of the historical hallmarks of family therapy practice has been the tendency to equate change with maximizing the involvement of family members in the therapy process.

Similarly, the remaining three items comprising the A-traditionalism factor prescribe practices that are out of the mainstream of traditional views about clinical practice. All three emphasize the responsibility of the therapist for directing the course of therapy, with the fourth item also operationalizing the therapeutic paradox by suggesting a therapist "can facilitate change in the family by exaggerating the problem behavior."

Interestingly, while the first-item loading on this factor might not be out of the mainstream for a therapist oriented to the Bowenian perspective, the same also may be true for the last three items and structural/strategic therapists. Indeed, as we have seen in our review of the development of family therapy practice, ideas that at one time were "a-traditional" or out of the mainstream may become institutionalized as a profession grows and diversifies. At the same time, as we also have seen in our previous analysis of the Insight and Professional Growth factors, ideas that have their roots or origins in other therapeutic modalities may exhibit a "conversion process" through which they become incorporated into emerging modalities within the family therapy enterprise.

Systemic View.   The item mean for the four items comprising the Systemic View factor was 2.96. Unquestionably this factor was rated "least descriptive" of their practice by the 713 family therapists responding to the Family Therapist's Assumption Scale. Indeed, Systemic View was the only factor on which the item mean fell within the "not descriptive" range on the six-point measurement scale.

An examination of the five items comprising this factor does not explain the relatively low score obtained; in fact, since each item suggests the application of propositions from general systems theory to family therapy, we might have expected this factor to represent the most heavily endorsed belief system. While, as in the case of the Problem-Solving factor, bivariate data analysis may clarify the underendorsement of this factor, we might offer two interpretations at this point.

The first explanation for the relatively low item mean for the Systemic View factor suggests that either there has been a breakdown in the "ripple effect" by which practitioners from one generation pass on their practice views to the next, or that it is still too early to measure the influence of this effect. In the case of the former it may be that, while a systemic view of family relationships guided the early development of the field, its influence has declined among contemporary practitioners. In the more likely case of the latter explanation, it may be that the propositions of general systems theory are not yet grounded in the practice strategies of this national sample of family therapists.

A second explanation for the relatively low item mean for the Systemic View factor is concerned with the items comprising the factor. While the logic of each item is consistent with general systems thinking, the items may not represent the most generic constructs by which systems thinking may be operationalized. Indeed, given the lack of consensus among family therapists about the precise meaning of a "systemic view," and consequently the identification of specific propositions representing the application of system theory to family practice, the measurement of the influence of "system thinking" may remain problematic for years to come.

Fortunately we shall have an opportunity to examine both the "ripple effect" and the measurement explanation for the low item mean on the Systemic View factor. As with the Problem-Solving factor, the meaning of this factor should become clearer as we proceed with an examination of the relationship between our subjects' theoretical orientation and their responses on the Family Therapist's Assumption Scale.

Family Therapist's In-session Style Inventory

The 26 items comprising the original Family Therapist's In-session Style Inventory also were factor analyzed following the same procedures described in the preceding section. As a result of our analysis, all but two of the original style items were retained in one of six extracted style factors. The name as well as the constituent items and their respective factor loadings are summarized in Table 3–2. As in the case of the assumption factors, item means for each style factor were calculated for each respondent by dividing the sum of the scores for each item in a given factor by the total number of items loading on that factor. Consequently, the range of factor scores for all of the style factors, like the assumption factors, was from 1 to 6. We now will describe and discuss each of the style factors in descending order, beginning with the factor receiving the highest item mean on the six-point scale (Attender) and ending with the factor receiving the lowest (Agitator).

Attender. The factor that was seen as most descriptive of their practice by the 751 responding family therapists was the Attender. The item mean for the five items comprising this factor was 4.79. The strength of the family therapists' endorsement of this factor is reflected in the fact that over 96 percent fell on the "descriptive" side of the scale (scores greater than 3).

The five items that comprise this factor stress the importance of attending to the feelings and behavior of families during therapeutic interventions. Similar factors have emerged repeatedly from previous empirical studies of the styles of practitioners of individually oriented psychotherapy (Sundland, 1977). Indeed, the landmark studies on the "core conditions" of the therapeutic relationship (Carkhuff, 1980; Rogers, Gendlin, Kiesler, & Truax, 1967; Truax & Carkhuff, 1967) add further credibility to the linkage between these factors and individual-oriented psychotherapy.

TABLE 3-2 Style Factors and Item Loadings:
National Survey.

Factor	Factor Loading
Factor I: Attender	
Listening	.75
Observing	.60
Reflecting	.46
Consistent	.34
Supporting	.30
Factor II: Modeler	
Reality testing	.52
Participating	.46
Modeling	.40
Persisting	.38
Factor III: Prober	
Analyzing	.71
Interpreting	.68
Neutralizing	.34
Questioning	.30
Factor IV: Detoxifier	
Comic	.75
Casual	.54
Improvising	.43
Factor V: Director	
Organizing	.66
Planning	.62
Arbitrating	.50
Directing	.38
Teaching	.31
Factor VI: Agitator	
Provoking	.76
Agitating	.70
Confronting	.47

While rooted in individual therapy, the structural family therapy model's emphasis on "joining skills" (Minuchin, 1974; Minuchin & Fishman, 1981) also clearly underlines the importance of such an action system for family therapists. Indeed, the relatively passive nature of the interventive behaviors that comprise this factor (e.g., listening, observing) has a particular empirical precedent in the family therapy literature. As we discussed in the preceding chapter, Beels and Ferber's landmark study (1969) of preeminent family therapists of the late 1960s suggested two predominant but polar styles. The "reactor" group of therapists, corresponding to our Attender style, were viewed as having less compelling public personalities than their opposite type, the conductors. Consequently, the "reactors" tended to respond to rather than initiate action during the course of therapy. Clearly, such a profile is mirrored by the items comprising the Attender.

Less understandable than the presence of the Attender style in our findings, however, is the magnitude of its endorsement by the responding family therapists. Indeed, there was no trend in our literature review that suggested that therapeutically reactive styles were more characteristic of the field than the more proactive interventions. Furthermore, it might be argued that one of the more visible contributions of the family therapy movement has been to increase the "activity level" of the therapist within the treatment process. Interestingly, however, like the most highly rated assumption factor (Insight), and unlike some of the less highly rated style factors we will discuss later, the therapeutic action system portrayed by the Attender factor appears to reflect the same "conversion process" discussed previously, whereby therapeutic principles and/or processes rooted in the traditions of individually oriented psychotherapy have been incorporated within the family therapy enterprise, as well.

Modeler.   The second most strongly endorsed style factor was the Modeler. The item mean for the four items comprising this factor was 4.38. The items in this factor tend to stress therapeutic activities that encourage the family members' emulation of the therapist. Consequently, this factor represents the more active stance toward the conduct of therapy that was minimized by the Attender factor.

The presence of the Modeler factor in this sample of family therapists, as well as the rather high relative endorsement of the items comprising this factor, are quite consistent with the profiles of family therapy action systems described in Chapter 2. Indeed, one of the action systems on which our literature review suggested convergence across models of family therapy was that of the therapist as a family life educator. Both Foley (1974) and Guerin (1976) concluded that one generic role of the family therapist is that of a teacher about family relationships. Although some family therapy models may prescribe more implicit teaching (Guerin, 1976), others, like Satir's communications model (Satir, 1967) formalize this role. Indeed, the items comprising the Modeler factor (reality testing, participating, modeling, and persisting) may represent more formalized teaching through therapeutic role modeling for family members.

Prober. The item mean for each of the remaining four style factors was below 4. Of these remaining factors, the Prober was rated the highest ($\bar{x} = 3.98$). Collectively, the four items forming this factor stress an action system that involves therapeutic inquiry, interpretation, and analysis. Like the Attender, the items that comprise this factor, and in particular the two highest loading items (analyzing and interpreting), represent therapeutic behaviors with a long historical tradition in the practice of psychodynamically oriented psychotherapy. Indeed, the analytic and interpretive therapeutic styles reflected in this factor may be linear extensions of the Attender (assessment/diagnosis) factor.

Detoxifier. The three items comprising the Detoxifier factor had an item mean of 3.79, ranking this factor fourth among the six style factors extracted. Collectively, the casualness, the humor, and the improvisation suggested by these items seem to portray activities that seek to relieve tension and anxiety in family members. Presumably, the function of such activities is to provide a climate or context whereby dialogue, learning, and modification of undesirable behavior may transpire.

Perhaps not unlike our findings for the A-traditionalism assumption factor, the relatively moderate item mean for this factor may reflect the mixing of divergent forces or viewpoints regarding the therapeutic process. On the one side we might find support for such a style in the casual, almost laid-back approach of Murray Bowen as well as in the sublime satire of Carl Whitaker. Yet, on the other side, we would find proponents of "shaking the system up," such as Salvadore Minuchin and Jay Haley. As with many of our findings thus far, we anticipate that greater clarity regarding the meaning of the items comprising the Detoxifier style factor will emerge when we explore areas of convergence and divergence between the three family therapy models.

Director and Agitator. The Director and the Agitator were, respectively, the fifth- and sixth-ranked style factors. The item mean for the five items loading on the Director factor was 3.70, while the three items comprising the Agitator were ranked last with a 3.36 item mean.

While the items comprising the Director stress the therapist's responsibility for the conduct of treatment and those loading on the Agitator factor stress disequilibrating activities on the part of the therapist, the two factors share a certain similarity. Just as the Attender and Prober may represent, as we have discussed, action systems that are rather congruent with the traditional therapeutic action systems of individual-oriented practitioners, the Director and the Agitator may represent rather a-traditional patterns of therapeutic intervention. With regard to the Director, the items suggest a therapeutic agent who is "in charge" of the process. Indeed, the therapeutic control suggested by these items is consistent with the "conductor" profile developed by Beels and Ferber (1969). Similarly, while the "provoking," "agitating," and "confronting" styles that comprise the Agitator factor may reflect an action system intent on breaking up unhealthy family patterns, they also stand in rather stark contrast to the more traditional styles represented by the Attender and the Modeler factors.

Finally, we would propose that the same lag in the "ripple effect" that we suggested as an explanation for the surprisingly low item mean for the Systemic View assumption factor also may be operating to explain the fact that the Director and Agitator were the two lowest rated style factors. Further reflection on the profession's segmentation process adds credence to this thesis, as we can note readily the convergence of systems-oriented models of family therapy (Gurman & Kniskern, 1981), as well as the directing and agitating therapeutic styles that surround the overlapping structural/strategic models of family therapy (Hoffman, 1981). In effect, therefore, what we may be seeing from our data thus far are two parallel forces: family therapists' inclusion of certain principles and processes that have their roots in traditional individual-oriented therapeutic models, as well as their (relative) exclusion of other principles and processes whose roots, while in the emerging family therapies, are (assumedly) yet to flower.

Personality Inventory (16PF)

As a starting point, we might note that there was little variability evidenced by the 418 family therapists who responded to this personality inventory. With a standardized scale range of zero to 26 points, the most descriptive personality attributes for this national sample were Self-assured, with a factor mean of 17.49, followed by Trusting (17.38) and Emotional Stability (16.23). The least descriptive personality attributes were Conscientious (13.16), Imaginative (13.24), and Happy-go-lucky (13.28). This rather narrow range from the most descriptive to least descriptive personality attributes perhaps will become more informative as we move to a comparative analysis of the three family therapy models in a later section of this chapter.

Comparing the Family Therapy Models: A Preliminary Analysis

To identify areas of convergence and divergence across the three selected models of family therapy, our initial data analysis utilized the revised Theoretical Orientation Scale to correlate the respondents' strength of theoretical orientation to each of the three models of family therapy with the three major data sets—assumption factors, style factors, and personality factors.

Assumption Factors

When we examined the results of the correlational analysis of strength of theoretical orientation to each model and each of the five assumption factors, significant correlation coefficients emerged for each model. Beginning with the communications model, three significant correlation coefficients were obtained. The highest of these emerged for the Insight factor ($r = .417; p < .001$), followed by the Professional Growth factor ($r = .378; p < .001$) and, at a substantially lesser magnitude, the Problem Solving factor ($r = .160; p < .001$). We did not find, however, statistically significant correlation coefficients for the relationship between strength of theoretical orientation to the communications model and the Systemic View and A-traditionalism assumption factors.

Three significant correlation coefficients also were obtained between the measure of theoretical orientation to the structural/strategic model and the assumption factors, although the magnitude of these coefficients generally was lower than those for the communications model. The highest of these significant coefficients was for the A-traditionalism factor ($r = .288; p < .0001$). The next highest coefficient revealed a weak but negative association for the Insight factor ($r = -.166; p < .0001$), while the weakest significant correlate was the Systemic View factor ($r = .150; p < .001$). Nonsignificant associations emerged for the Professional Growth and, perhaps surprisingly, the Problem Solving factor.

Only one assumption factor (Insight) was *not* significantly associated with strength of theoretical orientation to the Bowenian model. Of the four significant correlates, however, only one, Systemic View ($r = .390; p < .0001$), demonstrated any strength. Indeed, the coefficients for Professional Growth ($r = .164; p < .0001$), A-traditionalism ($r = .146; p < .001$), and Problem Solving ($r = -.084; p < .05$) reflected only negligible associations.

Collectively, the patterning of these correlation coefficients suggests a certain "face validity" with the family therapy literature. As the literature has suggested, patterns of both convergence and divergence characterize the empirical referents of the three models. Indeed, a concern with client insight distinguishes the communications model, while the de-emphasis of this factor unites the structural/strategic and Bowenian models. Similarly, as reflective of the writings of these family therapy exemplars, a concern with the professional/personal growth issue unites the communications and Bowenian models and confirms the lesser concern of the structural/strategic model with this variable.

With regard to our earlier identification of the communications model as the "most popular," the convergence of the structural/ strategic and Bowenian models in devaluing Insight and valuing the A-traditional assumption factors may be informative. Indeed, both of these patterns of association may reflect a movement away from adherence to historically traditional psychotherapeutic norms. If this is the case, the data also may be suggesting that the communications model is more readily reconciled with these norms. We shall come back to this point as we move beyond this preliminary stage of data analysis.

Style Factors

While the correlational analysis of the assumption factors provided relatively clear identifying belief systems on which the three models diverged as well as joined with one another, the correlation coefficients for the six style factors provide less information, both within and across models.

For the communications model, significant associations emerged for all six style factors. Overall, this pattern suggests little discriminability and consequently a rather vague profile of the communications model's action system. However, the two style factors that correlated the highest with adherence to the communications model, Modeler ($r = .342$; $p < .0001$) and Attender ($r = .286$; $p < .0001$), certainly reflect the writings of Satir and her associates. The range of association for the remaining four style factors was from .094 (Detoxifier) to .17 (Agitator).

The correlation coefficients between the style factors and strength of theoretical orientation to the structural/strategic approach were quite similar to those that emerged from the analysis of the communications model's styles. Five of the six were significantly correlated with orientation to the structural/strategic approach. Despite the relatively high value this model places upon interventive techniques for restructuring family systems, however, the magnitude of associations was quite low. The highest correlate was Agitator ($r = .230$; $p < .0001$), while the lowest was Detoxifier ($r = .116$; $p < .05$). Only the Attender factor was not significantly correlated with strength of adherence to this model, while the Prober factor was negatively associated ($r = -.123$; $p < .001$).

Similar to the other models, the correlational analysis of the style factors for the Bowenian model produced only minimal information. Although four of the six style factors were significantly associated with strength of theoretical orientation (Agitator, Prober, Modeler, and Detoxifier), the highest correlation coefficient obtained was but .133 for Agitator.

Assumption and Style Factors Combined

Taken together, three patterns emerge from the preliminary analysis of belief and action systems. First, the six style factors provide a generally weaker descriptive association with each of the three theoretical orientations to family therapy when compared to the descriptive power of the five assumption factors. Second, these same style factors also provide relatively weaker clues as to *what is distinctive about any particular model of family therapy*. This is perhaps best exemplified by the fact that strength of orientation to the communications model displayed statistically significant positive associations with all six style factors. Finally, because of this weaker access, these style factors also suggest that convergence, not divergence, between these three family therapy models is the prevailing pattern. Indeed, for half of the style factors (Agitator, Modeler, and Detoxifier), orientation to all three models displayed statistically significant positive associations. In summary, clearly this preliminary analysis indicates that practicing family therapists' statements about their "belief systems" provide a more descriptive and discriminating picture of the three models of family therapy than do their self-descriptive statements about their "action systems" in the actual practice of family therapy.

Personality Attributes

Finally, when we compared the three models of family therapy on the personality attributes possessed by their respective adherents, it is perhaps surprising to find that relatively few statistically significant associations appear and that they are, in fact, quite weak as well. In terms of divergence across the three models of family therapy, orientation to the communications model was significantly and positively associated with Outgoing ($r = .153$; $p < .02$) and Emotional Stability ($r = .149$; $p < .02$), while it was significantly and negatively associated with Imaginative ($r = .160$; $p < .01$). Orientation to the structural/strategic model diverged from orientation to the other two models by correlating positively with the personality attributes of Experimenting ($r = .169$; $p < .01$) and Self-assured ($r = .191$; $p < .005$). Finally, while orientation to the Bowenian model evidenced no distinctive or divergent personality trait associations, it did share a positive association with strength of orientation to the communications model on Venturesome ($r = .120; p < .05$). There were no statistically significant associations shared by both the strength of orientation to the Bowenian and the structural/strategic models.

In summarizing the findings from all three data sets, Table 3–3 portrays areas of convergence and divergence across the three models of family therapy, based upon statistical associations between strength of theoretical orientation and the assumption, style, and personality factors.

Comparing the Family Therapy Models: "High-group" Analysis

The measures of association between strength of theoretical orientation and the assumption, style, and personality factors presented in the previous section provide only a partial strategy for identifying areas of convergence and divergence across these three models of family therapy. Besides the fact that in correlational data statistical significance is highly influenced by sample size, such a strategy also permits inferences only about the actual between-group differences in the three models' respective means on any particular variable (factor). Finally, it also should be recognized that some of the respondents may have scored (relatively) high on the Theoretical Orientations Scale's subscale items for more than one family therapy model, thereby diluting the power of our analysis plan's attempt to discriminate among these three models.

In an effort to correct for these limitations and thereby provide a more sensitive and discriminating analysis of divergence and convergence across the field of family therapy, we selected three "high groups" from the pool of respondents, each representing one of the three models of family therapy under investigation. To create these three high groups, the most efficient decision rule was utilized: Only those respondents who scored *above* the mean for that particular model's Theoretical Orientations Scale subscale items, and *below* the mean for each of the other two models' subscales, were assigned to the appropriate family therapy model. The results of this procedure indicated that a reasonably selective group of family therapy practitioners was assigned to each of the high groups representing the three models of family therapy. In all, less than one-third of the entire

TABLE 3-3 Relationship between Theoretical Orientation and Assumption, Style, and Personality Factors: Profiling Divergence and Convergence.

Factors	Divergence			Convergence
	Communications	Structural/Strategic	Bowenian	
Assumptions				
Insight	(+)	(−)	ns	None
Problem Solving	(+)	ns	(−)	None
Professional Growth	(+)	ns	(+)	C + B
Systemic View	ns	(+)	(+)	S/S + B
A-traditionalism	ns	(+)	(+)	S/S + B
Styles				
Attender	(+)	ns	ns	S/S + B
Prober	ns	(−)	ns	C + B
Director	(−)	(+)	ns	None
Agitator				All
Modeler				All
Detoxifier				All
Personality				
Outgoing	(+)	ns	ns	S/S + B
Intelligent				All
Emotional Stability	(+)	ns	ns	S/S + B
Assertive				All
Happy-go-lucky				All
Conscientious				All
Venturesome	(+)	ns	(+)	C + B

(continued)

TABLE 3-3 (continued)

Factors	Divergence			Convergence
	Communications	Structural/Strategic	Bowenian	
Personality (continued)				
Tenderminded				All
Trusting				All
Imaginative	(−)	ns	ns	S/S + B
Forthright	(−)	ns	(−)	C + B
Self-assured	ns	(+)	ns	C + B
Experimenting	ns	(+)	ns	C + B
Self-sufficient				All
Controlled				All
Relaxed				All

Key: (+) symbol indicates a statistically significant (*p* < .05) *positive* association.
(−) symbol indicates a statistically significant (*p* < .05) *negative* association.
(ns) symbol indicates *no* statistical association. Blank cells also indicate no statistical association.

original national sample was retained, with 13.4 percent of the respondents assigned exclusively to the communications model's high group, and 8.2 percent of the respondents assigned to each of the remaining two models' high groups.

A brief composite profile of the respondents selected for this high-group subsample indicates that a total of 357 subjects were included in these three mutually exclusive high groups. This subsample's average age was 42.2 years, and over two-thirds (68.9%) were males. With regard to professional experience, most (82.5%) had their master's degree and almost one-half (43.1%) had their doctorates. In terms of practice experience, the high-group respondents averaged 9.6 years of family therapy practice, 9.4 years of individual practice, as well as almost five years of group therapy practice. Finally, they also were involved in a number of training-related activities, averaging 4.3 years as clinical supervisors, 2.8 years in staff development, and 2.5 years in university teaching. Overall, it is perhaps surprising to note that this composite demographic profile of the high group respondents was strikingly similar to the profile of the entire AAMFT/AFTA national sample.

Professional/Practice Activities

In an attempt to provide a more detailed profile and analysis of the high-group respondents' backgrounds and practice activities, between-group comparisons also were performed. With regard to demographic and experiential data, the profile consistently indicates that the structural/strategic model's high group was a clinically less experienced group than the communications and Bowenian models' high groups. The structural/strategic group averaged 39.1 years of age, as compared to 43.4 years for the other two groups ($p < .0004$), and averaged significantly fewer years of experience in practicing family therapy (just over 7 years, as compared to over 10 years; $p < .03$), individual therapy (6.3 years, as compared to approximately 10.5 years; $p < .002$), and group therapy (3.2 years, as compared to 5.5 years; $p < .03$). We also might note that in the paired comparisons of these data, the communications model's high group consistently scored above the Bowenian model's high group as well, although these findings were not always statistically significant.

This same pattern also emerges when we look at the respondents' educational level. Approximately 85 percent of the communications and Bowenian models' high-group respondents had master's degrees, as compared to 73.8 percent for the structural/strategic model's high group ($p < .02$). No significant differences emerged, however, with regard to the proportion of respondents in each of the three groups holding doctorates (averaging 43.1% for the entire sample), or for their number of years of experience in the practice of clinical supervision (averaging 4.3 years), staff development (2.8 years), teaching (2.5 years), or research (1.8 years).

With regard to a profile of the respondents' *current* practice activities, the structural/strategic model's group spent a significantly higher percentage of their current time in the practice of family therapy (36.0% of their time, as compared to 32.7% for the Bowenian group and only 25.8% for the communications group; $p < .01$), and in providing clinical supervision (10.0%, as compared to 8.5% and 5.9% for the Bowenian and communications groups, respectively; $p < .01$). On the other hand, they devoted a significantly lower percentage of their current time practicing individual therapy (26.3%, as compared to 39.0% for the Bowenian group and 36.6% for the communications group; $p < .01$). In addition, for all but one of these seven professional activities, the communications and Bowenian models' respondents expended similar proportions of their time, differing only in the amount of time devoted to group therapy (9.2% for the communications group, as compared to only 4.5% for the Bowenian group; $p < .01$).

Another descriptor of these high-group respondents' current practice activities was the average length of their cases. Here, we found that the communications and structural/strategic models' respondents joined in providing significantly more short-term therapy. Over one-third (approximately 38.0%) of their cases were seen in a three-month time period or less, whereas the Bowenian model's respondents saw less than one-fourth (22.4%) of their cases within this time period ($p < .0001$). On the other hand, it was not surprising that we found that the Bowenian respondents saw over one-fourth (27.6%) of their cases for more than one year, as compared to approximately only one-tenth for both the communications and structural/strategic groups ($p < .001$).

With regard to the units of treatment seen in their current practice, the structural/strategic group was significantly *less* likely to see only one of the parents or only the identified client/child, and significantly *more* likely to see the entire family, as compared to both the communications and Bowenian models' groups. Bowenian respondents, on the other hand, were significantly *less* likely to see the marital couple, as compared to the other two groups. Based upon the Bowenian model's preference for working with the marital couple and excluding children from therapy, we are somewhat surprised by this particular finding. It should be noted, however, that the *preferred* unit of treatment for all three high groups was the marital couple, with the major difference being that the communications and Bowenian respondents' alternative preferred unit was the adult spouse, while the structural/strategic respondents' alternative preferred unit of treatment was the whole family. All three groups, however, indicated that approximately one-half of their current cases did not include children as part of treatment. Interestingly, we found that the structural/ strategic respondents' statements on their preferred units of treatment were strongly consistent with the data on their actual current practice, in contrast to the communications and Bowenian models' respondents, who preferred seeing the family as a whole above seeing the parent/spouse alone but whose actual current practice caseloads showed just the opposite trend.

When we asked the respondents to define the nature of the identified problems in their current caseloads, the structural/strategic model's high group indicated that a significantly greater proportion of their cases were child-focused (24.5%, as compared to approximately 16.5% for the other two groups; $p < .01$). On the other hand, there were no marked differences between the respondents in the percentage of cases identified as marital problems (the entire sample averaged 44.6%) or parenting problems (11.0%).

With regard to the first finding, we are not surprised by the structural/strategic model's respondents' greater propensity to identify problems as child-focused. Its concern for a family's hierarchical structure and its goal of correcting distorted parental roles and authority patterns (i.e., putting the parents "in charge") logically would appear to focus attention upon the behavioral problems of children that tend to "reverse" the hierarchical alignments within the family. Nonetheless, it is surprising that we found no significant differences in the incidence of problems defined as parenting problems and, further, that this was the least prevalent problem identified across all three groups of respondents. Interestingly, when these family therapists were asked to isolate the family subsystem that reflected the most prevalent focus of their treatment, all three groups selected marital problems in almost half the cases. We might note that the marital couple also was the preferred unit of treatment by all three groups, perhaps raising an interesting question as to the way in which family therapists' definition of the problem may be influenced by their preferred treatment modalities and/or approaches.

Finally, with regard to the respondents' current practice, we found that the three models' high groups did not differ significantly in their use of cotherapists (this occurred in only 7.2% of the total cases), or in their frequency of seeing clients on a once-a-week basis (the composite average was 65.8% of the cases). The relatively infrequent involvement of cotherapists is not a particularly surprising finding. As we noted in Chapter 2, Bowen's concern with avoiding the triangulation process militates against its usage. Similarly, Haley's concern with reducing the concurrent involvement of "helping professionals" in a given family's life reflects an effort to avoid undermining the authority of the (primary) therapist. With regard to the relatively high frequency of cases seen on a once-a-week basis, on the other hand, we again may be seeing the same overlay of the more traditional individual-oriented therapy models that we observed in our earlier discussion of these respondents' belief and action systems.

Table 3–4 summarizes some of the key differences in the current practice activities of the three high groups, with *post hoc* paired comparisons performed to test statistically for areas of convergence and divergence among the three family therapy models.

Personality Attributes (16PF)

When we compare the three high groups on the 16 personality factors, the overwhelming pattern is one of convergence. While the smaller high-group sample sizes provided by this form of the questionnaire may have contributed to nonsignificant findings, Beels & Ferber's (1969) earlier assertions about the relationship between personality characteristics and theoretical orientations of family therapists are not reflected in our national sample. Indeed, on 14 of the 16 personality traits tested, the respondents in the three high groups displayed "pure" convergence or statistically nonsignificant differences in their factor means. The two exceptions were Assertive and Self-assured, where the communications model's respondents scored significantly lower than both the structural/strategic and Bowenian models' respondents ($p < .05$).

Belief Systems (Assumption Factors)

In Table 3–5 we compare the three high groups' item means on the five assumption factors, with *post hoc* paired comparisons performed to test statistically for areas of convergence and divergence among the three family therapy models.

An initial profiling indicates that both the communications and the Bowenian models' groups scored highest on Insight and Professional Growth, while the structural/strategic model's group scored highest on A-traditionalism. This pattern of findings paralleled the results of our preliminary correlation analysis for the communications and

TABLE 3-4 Comparison of High Groups on Selected Current Practice Activities.

Current Practice Activities	Communications (%)	Theoretical Orientations		Divergence[a]
		Structural/Strategic (%)	Bowenian (%)	
Proportion of Current Time				
Family therapy	25.77	36.02	32.72	S/S > C
Individual therapy	36.62	26.28	39.04	C + B > S/S
Proportion of Caseloads				
Less than 3 months	37.14	38.50	22.35	C + S/S > B
3–6 months	27.63	23.77	20.98	C > B
6–12 months	15.90	16.66	23.29	B > C + S/S
Over 1 year	10.15	9.53	27.62	B > C + S/S
Proportion of Caseloads				
Spouse only	17.83	13.43	21.26	C + B > S/S
Child only	4.69	5.62	4.90	ns
Marital couple	38.21	32.73	29.33	C + S/S > B
Whole family	13.55	23.84	18.14	S/S > C + B
Children only	3.13	1.44	1.93	C > S/S
Proportion of Caseloads				
Marital problem	48.08	40.19	43.59	C > S/S
Child-focused problem	15.40	24.54	17.96	S/S > C + B
Parenting problem	12.12	10.54	9.77	ns

[a]Post hoc paired comparisons; $p < .05$.

TABLE 3-5 Comparison of High Groups on Assumption Factors.

| Assumption Factors[a] | Theoretical Orientation | | | Convergence[b] | Divergence[b] |
	Communications	Structural/Strategic	Bowenian		
Insight	5.05	4.19	4.65	None	C > B > S/S
Professional Growth	4.82	4.02	4.51	C = B	C + B > S/S
Systemic View	2.67	2.89	3.18	C = S/S S/S = B	B > C
Problem Solving	4.26	3.98	3.88	C = S/S = B	None
A-traditionalism	3.95	4.44	4.01	C = B	S/S > C + B

[a]Factor scores represent standardized item means, utilizing a scale of 1 (strongly disagree) to 6 (strongly agree).
[b]Post hoc paired comparisons; $p < .05$.

structural/strategic models' adherents, but did not for the Bowenian model's adherents. More specifically, for the communications model's respondents, Insight and Professional Growth were also the highest correlates of orientation to that model. Similarly, the A-traditionalism factor was the highest correlate of orientation to the structural/strategic model. For the Bowenian model's respondents, on the other hand, Insight was the highest valued belief system for the high group sample, but was the only assumption factor that displayed a nonsignificant association to strength of adherence to this model in the preliminary correlational analysis for the less selective national sample.

Additional shifts in the within-group assumption parameters, when comparing our preliminary correlational analysis to the high-group analysis, also were particularly noteworthy, albeit problematic, for both the structural/strategic and Bowenian models. With regard to the structural/strategic model, for example, the Insight factor was negatively correlated to strength of adherence to this model in the preliminary analysis, but quite surprisingly ranked second highest in the more selective high-group analysis. Clearly, despite the writings of both Minuchin and Haley, among others, it would appear that the traditional psychotherapeutic belief system represented by this factor is alive and well among our national sample of family therapists.

And, with regard to the Bowenian model, perhaps the most striking shift is evidenced in the Systemic View factor. In our preliminary correlational analysis this factor displayed the strongest (positive) association with strength of adherence to this model. In our high-group analysis, however, this same factor was the lowest ranked for adherents of the Bowenian model.

With regard to convergence and divergence among the three models, "pure" convergence (statistically insignificant differences in item means across the three high groups) was achieved only on the Problem Solving assumption factor, whereas only the Insight factor achieved "pure" divergence (statistically significant differences in item means across all three groups). Partial convergence seemed most evident for the communications group, which overlapped (statistically insignificant item-mean differences) with the Bowenian group on three factors (Professional Growth, Problem Solving, and A-traditionalism), and with the structural/strategic group on two factors (Systemic View and Problem Solving). The structural/strategic and Bowenian high groups converged only on the Problem Solving assumption factor.

Overall, the findings displayed in Table 3–5 depict greater pure and partial *divergence* when compared to the inferred convergence/divergence presented in the preliminary correlational analyses. Consequently, the merit of using the more stringent definition (that is, the high-group analysis) of a practitioner's adherence to a particular theoretical orientation or model of family therapy appears to be affirmed. In addition, the profile of convergence and divergence shifts when comparing these two sets of findings. More specifically, Insight becomes a far more discriminating assumption factor, while Problem Solving becomes less so. For A-traditionalism, the communications and Bowenian model's high groups converge (diverging from the structural/strategic high group), whereas in the preliminary analysis the Bowenian model adherents converged with the structural/strategic model's adherents. For both the Systemic View and the Professional Growth assumption factors, the patterns of divergence/convergence in comparing the high-group analysis with the preliminary correlational analysis remained largely the same.

Action Systems (Style Factors)

In Table 3–6 we compare the three high groups' item means on the six style factors, with *post hoc* paired comparisons performed to test statistically for areas of convergence and divergence among the three family therapy models.

As in the case of the assumption factors, our high-group analysis of the style factors provides a more discriminating within-group profile for each model than did our preliminary correlational analysis. Also, as in the case of the assumption factors, we might note greater disparity between the results of the correlational analysis and the high group analysis for the structural/strategic and Bowenian models than for the communications model.

For example, the Attender and Modeler factors were the highest correlates of strength of theoretical orientation to the communications model in the correlational analysis *and* also the two most descriptive style factors for the Communications model's high-group respondents. With regard to both the structural/strategic and Bowenian models, however, the most descriptive style factor for their respective high-group respondents (Attender) was not significantly correlated with strength of theoretical orientation to either model in our preliminary analysis.

Perhaps two trends are most impressive when we survey the comparative findings in Table 3–6. First, respondents representing all three models rated the Attender style as most descriptive of their practice and rated the Agitator style as least descriptive. Indeed, by essentially controlling for theoretical orientation among the family

TABLE 3-6 Comparison of High Groups on Style Factors.

Style Factors[a]		Theoretical Orientation			
	Communications	Structural/Strategic	Bowenian	Convergence[b]	Divergence[b]
Attender	4.85	4.29	4.65	C = B	C + B > S/S
Director	3.60	3.66	3.40	C = S/S = B	None
Agitator	3.28	3.21	2.95	C = S/S = B	None
Prober	4.06	3.42	4.02	C = B	C + B > S/S
Modeler	4.35	3.97	3.95	S/S = B	C > S/S + B
Detoxifier	3.75	3.67	3.63	C = S/S = B	None

[a]Factor scores represent standardized item means, utilizing a scale of 1 (not descriptive) to 6 (very descriptive).
[b]Post hoc paired comparisons; $p < .05$.

therapy practitioners, the present findings tend to affirm further our interpretation of the univariate analysis. Clearly, the most characteristic belief system (Insight) and action system (Attender) are those more congruent or closely aligned with the practice of individual psychotherapy. The meaning of this trend, however, is less clear at this point. While it may suggest, as we mentioned earlier, a "generation gap" between the exemplars and practitioners of the three models, we will address this question empirically in Chapter 4.

A second trend in our high-group data suggests that there is far greater *convergence* among these three models of family therapy when comparing their respective action systems (style factors) than there is with their belief systems (assumption factors). Indeed, pure convergence (statistically insignificant differences among all three high groups' item means) appears for half of the six style factors: Director, Agitator, and Detoxifier. On the other hand, pure divergence appears on none of these six style factors. The Bowenian model's respondents, for example, identified *no* style factors on which they significantly diverged from the other two models' respondents. Indeed, the only areas of partial divergence appear wherein the structural/strategic group is significantly lower than the communications and Bowenian groups on both the Attender and Prober factors, while the communications group is significantly higher than the other two groups on the Modeler factor.

While the empirical evidence specifying the nature of the relationship between therapeutic belief and action systems is incomplete and at times confounded by questions about the predictive power of self-reported data in profiling what actually occurs in therapy (Sundland, 1977), we might offer two interpretations explaining the disparity between the patterning of divergence for assumptions and convergence for styles. On the one hand, if a therapist's belief system about family interaction defines and thereby guides or directs the stylistic nature of his interventions (Guerin, 1976; Madanes & Haley, 1977), our findings may indicate that the family therapy profession may be in a relatively early phase in the sequential pathway of its knowledge-building process. Indeed, there may be a gap between the clarity of the articulation of theoretical concepts and articulation of interventive techniques. In view of the rapid dissemination of books and journals about family therapy in the last 10 years and the likelihood that belief systems are acquired more easily than interventive techniques from the consumption of these sources of knowledge, the subsequent phase wherein a divergence in style or action systems evolves from the existent divergence in belief systems may yet await the wider accessibility and utilization of intensive training and research within each of the major approaches to family therapy.

On the other hand, as an alternative thesis for explaining the disparity between the patternings of divergence for assumptions and of convergence for styles, we might propose that the expected relationship between belief and action systems may be more tenuous than that suggested by the sequential model of knowledge building just outlined. From one perspective, it might be argued that the same belief system may be subject to a number of different stylistic interpretations, contingent on, for example, the age, experience, or personal attributes of the therapist. Similarly, it also might be argued that the family therapist inevitably has an easier time in adding interventive techniques to his action system than in adding assumptions about the process and goals of the therapeutic enterprise to his belief system. Greater convergence or overlap of styles than of beliefs is to be expected, then, when comparing the major approaches to family therapy. It stands to reason that theoretical orientation may always possess only limited or circumscribed influence on or predictive accuracy for the actual practice of family therapy.

In the context of the profession's increasing advocacy on behalf of determining a common theory of family interaction and intervention (Olson, Russell, & Sprenkle, 1980; Simon, 1980), the interpretation of the findings in this national sample of family therapists assumes particular significance. If, in fact, the sequential model of knowledge building applies, and particular interventive styles or action systems do conform to particular theories or belief systems about family interaction, then our data suggest that the search for commonalities across varying models of family therapy may be premature. If, however, belief systems only partially or inadequately direct or inform action systems, then the search for commonalities across approaches to family therapy becomes largely irrelevant when viewed in the broader context of the more urgent priority of determining linkages between specific intervention or action systems and therapeutic effectiveness or outcome.

A significant direction, therefore, and one to which we will turn in Chapter 4, is the evaluation of the linkages between the belief and action systems of family therapists who have been intensively trained in each of these three models of family therapy. If our first thesis is valid, we would expect to observe greater stylistic divergence within this selective population; whereas, if our second thesis is valid, stylistic convergence should continue to be the rule.

Summary

When used to compare practitioners oriented to each of the three models of family therapy under investigation, our analysis of convergence and divergence clearly demonstrated that the respondents' belief systems provided a more descriptive and discriminating profile of the uniqueness of each model than did their action systems. Furthermore, when we compared these results with the existing literature in the field, we found a far better "goodness of fit" for the five assumption factors. For example, our discussions of each exemplar in Chapters 1 and 2 clearly would have predicted that the Insight and Professional Growth factors would most vividly portray the orthogonal positions taken by Satir and Bowen on the one hand, and Minuchin and Haley on the other. Similarly, the structural/strategic model's adherents' stronger valuing of the A-traditionalism assumption factor once again is compatible with the literature, such as Haley's paradoxical views about the therapeutic process and the strong emphasis the exemplars of this model place upon the therapist's responsibility for directing the course of the clinical enterprise. Perhaps the most puzzling finding pertains to the Problem Solving assumption factor, however, and the lack of divergence across respondents representing these three family therapy models. The literature would suggest that the structural/strategic model's respondents would evidence the highest scores, but the lack of such findings might indicate that the exemplars of this model may view the Problem Solving assumption factor as being more descriptive of the therapist's orientation to treatment than of the family members' actual involvement or role in the therapeutic process.

The findings pertaining to the six style factors, on the other hand, provide such an overwhelming patterning of convergence across the three models of family therapy that it confounds our attempts to construct a reality test for the fidelity of our data with regard to the existing family literature. While we might have predicted, correctly, that the communications model's respondents would identify the Modeler interventive style as more descriptive of their practice, and that all three models of family therapy would strongly value the "joining skills" inherent in the Attender style factor, the pure convergence in the three models' respondents' ratings of the Director, Agitator, and Detoxifier interventive styles is particularly confusing and unanticipated. We would have predicted from the literature that the structural/strategic model's respondents would have scored highest on these first two style factors (and lowest on the third), while the

Bowenian model's respondents would have produced directionally opposite findings.

Overall, these findings may offer at least the hypothesis that the family therapy literature may serve as a better source or model for theoretical orientations or "belief systems" and that the practitioner's application or implementation of whichever theoretical orientation(s) he chooses becomes more diffuse or at least less prescribed when actual in-session interventive behaviors are mandated. When we interface this hypothesis with our findings that a more stringent or rigorous definition of adherence to a particular model of family therapy (the high-group analysis plan) produced more discriminating profiles for each model, we are led unalterably to the next most rigorous definition possible: practitioners who have received intensive training and supervision in each of these same three models of family therapy. It is to this group that we turn in the next chapter.

References

Beels, C. C., & Ferber, A. Family therapy: A view. *Family Process*, 1969, *8*, 280–332.

Bowen, M. *Family therapy in clinical practice.* New York: Jason Aronson, 1978.

Carkhuff, R. R. *The art of helping IV.* Amherst, Mass.: Human Resource Development Press, 1980.

Cattel, R. R., Eber, H. W., & Tatsuika, M. M. *Sixteen personality factor questionnaire.* Champaign, Ill.: Institute for Personality and Ability Testing, 1962.

Foley, V. D. *An introduction to family therapy.* New York: Grune and Stratton, 1974.

Guerin, P. J. *Family therapy: Theory and practice.* New York: Gardner Press, 1976.

Gurman, A. S., & Kniskern, D. P. (Eds.). *Handbook of family therapy.* New York: Brunner/Mazel, 1981.

Hoffman, L. *Foundations of family therapy.* New York: Basic Books, 1981.

Jones, S. L. *Family therapy: A comparison of approaches.* Bowie, MD: Brady, 1980.

Kerr, M. E. Family systems theory and therapy. In A. S. Gurman & D. P. Kniskern (Eds.), *Handbook of family therapy.* New York: Brunner/Mazel, 1981.

Madanes, C., & Haley, J. Dimensions of family therapy. *Journal of Nervous and Mental Disease*, 1977, *165*, 88–89.

Minuchin, S. *Families and family therapy.* Cambridge, Mass.: Harvard University Press, 1974.

Minuchin, S., & Fishman, H. C. *Family therapy techniques.* Cambridge, Mass.: Harvard University Press, 1981.

Napier, A. Y., & Whitaker, C. Problems of a beginning family therapist. In D.

A. Bloch (Ed.), *Techniques of psychotherapy*. New York: Grune and Stratton, 1973.

Olson, D. H., Russell, C. S., & Sprenkle, D. H. Marital and family therapy: A decade review. *Journal of Marriage and the Family*, 1980, 42, 973–994.

Rogers, C., Gendlin, E., Kiesler, D., & Truax, C. (Eds.). *The therapeutic relationship and its impact: A study of psychotherapy with schizophrenics*. Madison: University of Wisconsin Press, 1967.

Satir, V. A family of angels. In J. Haley & L. Hoffman (Eds.), *Techniques of family therapy*. New York: Basic Books, 1967.

Satir, V. *Peoplemaking*. Palo Alto, Calif.: Science and Behavior Books, 1972.

Simon, R. Conclusion of an interview with Salvadore Minuchin. *Family Therapy Practice Network Newsletter*, 1980, 3, 5–10.

Sundland, D. M. Theoretical orientations of psychotherapists. In A. Gurman & A. Razin (Eds.), *Effective psychotherapy*. New York: Pergamon Press, 1977.

Thaxton, L., & L'Abate, L. The "second wave" and the second generation: Characteristics of the new leaders in family therapy. *Family Process*, 1982, 21, 359–362.

Truax, C., & Carkhuff, R. *Toward effective counseling and psychotherapy: Training and practice*. Chicago: Aldine, 1967.

4

The Graduates of Family Therapy Training Programs

The survey of practicing family therapists presented in Chapter 3 provided a comparative exploration of areas of convergence and divergence among three of the major models of family therapy. In that survey, our sampling strategy (questionnaires mailed to AAMFT/ AFTA membership) largely dictated that, while the practice arena would be broadly scanned, the nature and depth of the respondents' exposure to each of the three models would be quite varied. Perhaps more important, this sampling strategy almost assured that in most instances the respondents' strength of theoretical orientation or adherence to a particular model of family therapy would be nurtured predominantly by their reading of the literature in the field. This perhaps might be augmented by some not-necessarily-systematic or intensive exposures to these models through attending one- or two-day workshops by a model's pioneer or disciple or through attending presentations at regional or national professional conferences.

In Chapter 2, however, one limitation of our national sampling strategy was identified in the GAP report (1970), where preference for a particular exemplar and/or model of family therapy was associated with geographic accessibility and visibility. In addition, our findings in Chapter 3 that a "poorness of fit" prevailed, when looking at the belief and action systems *within* each family therapy model, offered yet another limitation on this method. Indeed, our data suggested that emulation of an approach to family therapy that is based largely upon the existing and available literature may be easier to achieve at the conceptual or theoretical level than at the level of the actual interventive behaviors utilized in practice. To overcome these limitations, therefore, and to implement a more rigorous definition of family therapy theoretical orientation, we decided to survey practicing family therapists who had received intensive supervision at the training programs representing each of these three models of family therapy.

Methodology

The sampling plan for this "known-group" study of the graduates of the training programs was largely dictated by the way in which each of the three pioneers of the respective models of family therapy chose to define therapists intensively trained in their particular approach. For the structural/strategic and Bowenian models' respondents, graduates of their internship programs were selected. This procedure excluded persons on each institute's mailing list who had attended time-limited workshops or conferences and instead narrowly focused on those who had received ongoing supervision, typically of at least one year's duration, by the institute's staff and within the institute's facilities. We also should note that, while Chapter 2 documents the considerable degree of agreement as to the conceptually overlapping characteristics of the structural and the strategic models of family therapy, our sampling plan involved only interns graduating from Jay Haley and Cloe Madanes' Family Institute in Chevy Chase, Maryland, as representatives of this model of family therapy. The Philadelphia Child Guidance Clinic internship program's graduates were not sampled. Finally, the communications model's known-group sample was operationalized as members of Virginia Satir's Avanta Network, a grouping of family therapists whose collaborative personal and professional development activities do not interconnect around any particular geographically identifiable "training center" and typically are implemented in month-long retreats rather than weekly supervisory sessions. We should underscore, however, that our identification of practicing family therapists who were both extensively and intensively trained in each of these three models of family therapy was performed individually by each of the model's respective pioneers; hence, we are very appreciative of Murray Bowen, Jay Haley, and Virginia Satir for their assistance in making possible this second stage of our study of convergence and divergence within the field of family therapy.

This known-group study had one important additional variation from our national survey described in the previous chapter. In this study, all of the instrumentation was sent to all of the graduates on the three mailing lists. There were no separate, overlapping questionnaire forms. The data package therefore included the following: The Theoretical Orientation Scale, the Family Therapist's Assumption Scale, the Family Therapist's In-session Style Inventory, the 16PF, and demographic data questions. In addition, because of this questionnaire's length and the smaller population of graduates to which it was mailed, we carried out several follow-up mailings to ensure a return rate adequate for enabling statistical analyses of areas of convergence and divergence between these three models.

As a result, a total of 156 usable questionnaires was returned and included in this known-group study, representing a return rate for all three models of 62.8 percent. Forty-nine respondents comprised the communications model's known group (70% return rate), 70 comprised the Bowenian model's known group (56% return rate), and 37 comprised the structural/strategic model's known group (69% return rate).

While we will present a comparison of these three known groups on demographic data and current practice activities in a later section of this chapter, taken together the 156 respondents averaged 43.5 years of age, ranging from 27 to 74 years. They were an experienced group of practitioners, averaging 9.5 years of practice experience in family therapy, 5.9 years of working with individuals, and almost 4.0 years working with groups. In addition, they averaged 4.5 years of experience as clinical supervisors, 3.3 years in staff development activities, and 2.4 years in university instruction. Their educational backgrounds also were strong, with over four-fifths (82.8%) holding master's degrees and almost one-half (43.9%) holding doctorates. Of interest is the fact that the known-group respondents were predominantly female (66.8%). Finally, the respondents devoted a significant proportion (79.3%) of their current professional lives to clinical activities, predominantly providing family therapy (40.5%) and individual therapy (14.2%) but also engaging in a range of training-related activities such as clinical supervision (11.4%), staff development (7.6%), and teaching (3.0%).

Now let us take a closer look at the instrumentation. While we noted that the same instrumentation was used in this known-group study of the graduates of the three training programs as was utilized in the national survey presented in Chapter 3, differences in the use and composition of the instruments also should be noted. First, we did not use the Theoretical Orientation Scale to determine the respondents' theoretical orientation for between-group comparisons. Obviously, we knew each respondents' primary orientation *a priori*. However, since this instrument was constructed to provide a measure of each family therapist's degree of eclecticism as well as allegiance to one particular model, it was retained for use with the present sample. Second, we found that the factor analysis of the items from the Family Therapist's Assumption Scale and the Family Therapist's In-session Style Inventory produced somewhat different factor structures.

In this section, therefore, we utilize a *revised* Theoretical Orientation Scale to describe the strength of the respondents' orientation to the model in which they received training as well as to each of the other models of family therapy. In addition, we also detail the nature of the belief and action system factors created from the known-group respondents. Finally, we describe the known-group respondents with regard to the two major variables that remained the same, as described previously in Chapter 3: (1) personality factors derived from the 16PF, and (2) background data and current practice activities.

The Theoretical Orientation Scale

The known-group respondents averaged above a three on a six-point continuum for each of the three theoretical orientation scales. However, the average of the scores for strength of orientation to the Bowenian model (4.55) was considerably greater than that for orientation to either the communications (3.76) or the structural/strategic (3.81) model. These scores stand in rather strong contrast to the national sample, where orientation to the communications model clearly predominated. However, since the number of family therapists trained in and consequently representing the Bowenian model exceeded those representing each of the other models, these scores may be misleading.

A clearer picture of the strength of theoretical orientation of these known-group respondents emerged from our within-group analysis. For respondents representing each model, we obtained theoretical orientation scores for that model as well as for the other two models. As expected, known-group respondents scored significantly higher on the model in which they were trained than they did on the other models. Indeed, the scores for each model for therapists trained in that model were between five and six on the six-point scale. However, some major differences emerged when we examined the theoretical orientation scores of the respondents for those models in which they were *not* trained.

Interestingly, these within-group comparisons also may shed some additional light on our findings in Chapter 3 of the greater popularity of the communications model with respondents comprising our national sample. Indeed, while therapists representing both the structural/strategic and Bowenian known groups averaged precisely the same (3.02) on the scale measuring orientation to the communications model, the communications model respondents scored significantly higher than the Bowenian respondents on the structural/strategic scale ($p < .0001$) and significantly higher than the structural/strategic respondents on the Bowenian scale ($p < .0001$). While we will address the question of eclecticism in Chapter 6, the present findings may be pointing to a greater degree of theoretical diversity among the communications model respondents when compared to both the Bowenian and the structural/strategic models' respondents.

The Family Therapist's Assumption Scale

The 33 items constituting the original Family Therapist's Assumption Scale were subjected to factor analysis, employing an equimax rotation procedure. Assumption items loading at .35 or higher were retained, while items loading on two or more factors at .35 were initially excluded but then independently correlated with each constructed factor. Items still correlating with more than one factor then were dropped, while items correlating at .35 exclusively with only one factor were added. As a result of this procedure, 26 of the original 33 items loaded on one of seven assumption factors. Table 4–1 lists the names of each of these factors as well as their constituent assumption items and respective factor loadings.

Following the same methodology utilized to examine the belief systems characterizing the national sample, we first computed mean item scores for each of the seven assumption factors. Below, we describe and discuss each of these factors in descending order. We begin with *Role Structure*, the factor most strongly endorsed by the trainees of Bowen, Haley, and Satir, and end with *Family Responsibility*, the factor receiving the lowest mean item score from this known group sample.

Role Structure. The item mean for the two items comprising this factor was 4.53. Almost 85 percent of all known-group respondents scored above the scale's midpoint (3), and more than 30 percent of the family therapists rated both items with a 6, suggesting they "strongly agreed" with both assumptions comprising the Role Structure factor. Interestingly, neither item loaded on any of the five factors extracted from the national sample data.

TABLE 4–1 Assumption Factors and Item Loadings: Known-group Survey.

Factors	Factor Loadings
Factor I: Family Role Structure	
A therapist should respect and support the difference in authority inherent in the role structure of the family.	.73
A central focus of family therapy is one of clarifying the roles and relationships within and between the varying substances of the family.	.45
Factor II: Therapist as Facilitator	
Much of the process of family therapy focuses on the way in which family members send messages, the way in which family members receive and interpret these messages, and the difficulties arising from a lack of understanding between sender and receiver.	.71
By re-enacting or "mirroring" family members' patterns of relating, a family therapist can enable the family members to recognize their own behaviors and the impact of their behaviors on each other.	.68
Change in family members' behaviors can be effected by helping each member to deal with his/her feelings about self and about the other family members.	.58
Change in family members' feelings about themselves and each other can be effected by showing them alternative patterns of behaving.	.46
Factor III: Therapist as Theoretician	
An extensive family history should precede family treatment.	.58
Family therapy should be more concerned with the present than with the past.	–.57
Change in a family system can be effected when working with only one member of the family.	.53
A family therapist should avoid emotional interchanges among family members and focus on rational processes.	.52
A family member can best effect change in his/her patterns of relating to present family members by effecting change in the patterns of relating to his/her family of origin.	.50
Family therapy is not the appropriate model of intervention in all case situations.	–.47
Behind every child's problem is a marital problem.	.35

(continued)

TABLE 4-1 (continued)

Factors	Factor Loadings
Factor IV: Therapist as Risk-taker	
A family therapist should share his/her perceptions of verbal and nonverbal behavior with family members in order to enable better understanding of the impact of their behavior.	.64
Appropriate self-disclosure by the therapist is a vital part of the conduct of family therapy.	.56
The use of a cotherapist enhances the effectiveness of the conduct of family therapy.	.52
To be effective, the family therapist should provide alternative interpretations for family members' behaviors.	.45
Changes in family members' ways of relating can be effected by their learning new ways of relating to the family therapist.	.40
Family V: Family Participation	
Regardless of the nature of the presenting problem, all members of the family should be involved on a continuing basis in family therapy.	.56
Involving young children in family therapy hinders the conduct of the therapeutic process.	−.53
If a family member shares information with the family therapist, it should be shared with all members of the family.	.46
Factor VI: Therapist as Director	
To become effective as a family therapist, the use of video tape or the presence of the supervisor in the actual therapy sessions is essential.	.70
The family therapist ultimately is responsible for whether or not change occurs within a family.	.60
The therapist cannot avoid becoming an interacting member of the family system.	.39
Factor VI: Family Responsibility	
Responsibility for the content and conduct of the family therapy session should be assumed by the family members.	.65
A therapist should take responsibility for directing the course of family therapy.	−.60

Unlike the factor rated the highest by the national sample of family therapists (Insight), the items comprising this factor have no precedent in the practice of individual psychotherapy. Rather, the focus on the hierarchical divisions of responsibility in the family and, in particular, on the clarification of roles and relationships within and between the constituent subsystems of the family has been unique to the growth of the professional literature of family therapy. Indeed, as we suggested in Chapter 2, many of the early family therapy pioneers focused almost exclusively on either the distribution of power or on the nature of family roles at one time or the other during the early years of the family therapy movement. Consequently, the high endorsement of this factor by trainees of historically prominent family therapists was expected.

Therapist as Facilitator.   The item mean for the Therapist as Facilitator factor was 4.16. This is the only other assumption factor in the known-group sample for which a mean higher than 4.0 was obtained. In some respects the four items comprising this factor resemble the Insight factor extracted from the national sample. Indeed, three of the four items loading on the Therapist as Facilitator factor also loaded on the Insight factor. However, a closer scrutiny of this known-group factor suggests that the two factors represent different emphases. The thrust of the Therapist as Facilitator, while certainly emphasizing insight or understanding, is more toward the role of communication as an agent that facilitates new understandings among family members.

The emphasis on communication in the Therapist as Facilitator as opposed to the Insight factor perhaps is observed best from the respective factor loadings on an item that attempted to summarize the central communications proposition of the early Palo Alto group (Watzlawick, Beavin, & Jackson, 1967). This item (see Table 4–1) was stated: "Much of the process of family therapy focuses on the way in which family members send messages, the ways in which family members receive and interpret these messages, and the difficulties arising from a lack of understanding between sender and receiver." As can be observed in Table 3–1, the magnitude of the factor loading for this item was the lowest for all six items comprising the Insight factor. On the other hand, for the Therapist as Facilitator factor in the present known-group sample (Table 4–1), this communications theory axiom loaded higher than any of the other three items. Clearly, the thrust of the Therapist as Facilitator is on the type of insight that is developed through shared communications among family members and on the therapist's role in promoting this insight. Indeed, the remaining three items also suggest a "here-and-now" focus, with the therapeutic encounter directed toward family members learning new behaviors within the treatment context. Consequently, in both instances, like the Role Structure factor, the rather high ranking of the Therapist as Facilitator factor "squares" with the family therapy literature.

Therapist as Theoretician. The item mean for the seven items comprising the Therapist as Theoretician factor was 3.81, solidly on the "descriptive" side of the six-point scale. The major family therapy belief system represented by the clustering of these items is a dual one. Clearly, one of the thrusts is the use of a systems theory lens through which to view family theory and therapy. In fact, three of the seven items (the last three) also loaded on the Systemic View factor that emerged from the national sample of family therapists. However, unlike the Systemic View factor, the Therapist as Theoretician also incorporates an additional thrust that suggests that family history and antecedent events and dynamics play a role in defining current family interactions and in effecting changes in these patterns. This joint emphasis on systems thinking and family history is particularly congruent with our literature review in Chapter 2, which identified a number of family therapy typologies using these variables as parameters in defining the major schools of family therapy practice (Foley, 1974; Gurman & Kniskern, 1981; Hoffman, 1981; Jones, 1980; Madanes & Haley, 1977). Consequently, both the appearance and the high ranking of the Therapist as Theoretician factor in the known group is not surprising.

Therapist as Risk-taker. The item mean for the fourth-ranking assumption factor was 3.35. As summarized in Table 4–1, the five assumptions that comprise this Therapist as Risk-taker factor stress the family therapist's use of self. What becomes rather clear from an examination of these items, however, is that the particular "therapeutic self" reflected by these items stresses a more active role on the part of the therapist. What they seem to emphasize is the therapist's role as reality tester of current patterns of interaction as well as modeler of alternative patterns. Predominant therapeutic characteristics appear to be candor, honesty, and a willingness to risk personal self-disclosure when appropriate.

Family Participation. The three items comprising the Family Participation factor ranked fifth among the known-group respondents. The item mean was just barely on the "agree" side of the six-point scale (3.15). Indeed, a closer examination of the distribution of scores for this factor revealed that the item mean for the majority of responding family therapists (63.6%) was on the "disagree" (three or less) side of the scale. Since the practice of family therapy, at least as portrayed in the literature, historically has been characterized by increasing degrees of family participation in the treatment process, we would not have expected these low overall scores. On the other hand, as we discussed in Chapter 2, differential definitions of family therapy abound in the profession's literature. Indeed, some family therapists argue that the therapist's way of understanding human problems, rather than the presence of particular individuals in the treatment sessions, is the primary indicator of family therapy practice (Bowen, 1978; Olson, Russell, & Sprenkle, 1980). Therefore, we shall pay particular attention to differentials in the response to the items comprising Family Participation when we compare the belief systems across our three differentially trained groups of family therapists.

Therapist as Director. The item mean for the three items comprising the Therapist as Director factor was 3.10, quite similar to the score obtained for the Family Participation factor. Indeed, precisely the same percentage of respondents (63.6) averaged below the "agree" side of the scale. Collectively, the items comprising this sixth-ranked assumption factor stress the therapist's responsibility for both defining and guiding the course of therapy. Like the relatively low score obtained for the Family Participation factor, the items comprising the Therapist as Director factor probably were depressed by between-model variation. As we discussed in Chapter 2, the amount of control and responsibility assumed by the therapist is a central axis that typically has been utilized in typologies describing the various schools and models of family therapy. Finally, as discussed in Chapter 3, we also find the same seemingly paradoxical devaluing of the previous factor (Family Participation) while also devaluing the therapist-in-control stance reflected by this factor. Perhaps the meaning of these findings will become clearer as we move to our between-group comparisons of these three models of family therapy.

Family Responsibility. This final assumption factor is comprised by two items that stress the family members' responsibility for the course of family therapy. The item mean for this factor (2.1) was clearly in the disagree range of the scale. Only five of the 157 known-group respondents indicated they strongly agreed with these items (or strongly disagreed with the negatively loaded item), while almost a third (31.2%) indicated strong disagreement with these two assumptions by responding with the scale extreme. Once again, the same seemingly paradoxical stance as was taken in the low valuing of Therapist as Director beckons for explanation.

The Family Therapist's Style Inventory

Unlike the results of the factor analysis of the Family Therapist's Assumption Scale, the varimax rotation procedure employed with the

26 items comprising the Family Therapist's Style Inventory for the known-group respondents resulted in a factor structure that is remarkably similar to that which emerged from the national sample of family therapists. For the present sample, 25 of the 26 style items loaded exclusively on one of six factors representing the therapeutic action systems of these intensively trained family therapists. Interestingly, each of these style factors has a corresponding factor in the national sample. However, we find that the popularity or strength of endorsement of these factors is quite different across the two samples. While we examine the nature of these differences and explore some potential consequences and implications in Chapter 5, in this section we merely describe these known-group style factors. Table 4–2 summarizes each of the known-group factors and the items that comprise them, as well as their loadings.

The items comprising the *Attender* received the highest item mean (4.99) from our known-group sample. Clearly, this factor resembles the style factor of the same name in the national sample. Indeed, three of the four items that comprise this factor (listening, observing, and consistent) also loaded on the Attender factor in our data from the national sample. Consequently, the action system suggested by this factor also stresses a relatively passive or reactive therapeutic posture. This posture is responsive to the feelings and behaviors of family members while focusing on information retrieval.

The style factor that ranked second among our known-group respondents, the *Composer*, received an item mean of 4.15. This factor was comprised by three items, two of which loaded on the Detoxifier factor in the national sample. Consequently, while resembling the Detoxifier, the Composer suggests the additional dimension of therapeutic wisdom, capturing perhaps the somewhat aloof figure of the therapist as a "sage."

The factor that received the third highest endorsement (4.04) from our known-group respondents, the *Modeler*, mirrors the style factor with the same name in the data from the national sample. Indeed, three of the four items that loaded on this factor (participating, reality testing, and modeling) also loaded on the Modeler factor in our national sample of family therapists. Like its corresponding factor, the known-group Modeler stresses activities that encourage the family members' emulation of the family therapist as well as suggests an interactive and participatory style.

The item mean (4.04) for the fourth-ranked style factor, the *Planner*, was the same as that obtained for the Modeler. Comprised of three items, two of which (planning and organizing) also loaded on the

TABLE 4–2 Style Factors and Item
Loadings: Known-group Survey.

Factor	Factor Loading
Factor I: Attender	
Listening	.73
Questioning	.69
Observing	.67
Consistent	.45
Factor II: Composer	
Comic	.63
Casual	.62
Teaching	.46
Factor III: Modeler	
Participating	.67
Reality Testing	.60
Modeling	.57
Supporting	.43
Factor IV: Planner	
Planning	.70
Organizing	.64
Neutralizing	.36
Factor V: Analyzer	
Analyzing	.58
Interpreting	.57
Reflecting	.53
Factor VI: Energizer	
Provoking	.70
Confronting	.66
Agitating	.60
Reacting	.55
Persisting	.51
Arbitrating	.60
Expert	.42
Directing	.40

corresponding national sample style factor (the Director), this factor stresses a purposeful and goal-directed therapeutic style.

Item means for the fifth- and sixth-ranked style factors were the only ones to fall below four on the six-point scale, although they still were above the scale midpoint, meaning that both were "descriptive" of our known-group sample. The *Analyzer* (3.40) was ranked fifth and the *Energizer* (3.23) sixth. Comprised of three items, two of which (analyzing and interpreting) loaded previously on the Prober national sample factor, the Analyzer stresses therapeutic activities that serve to assess the dynamics presumed to underly interpersonal behaviors. Finally, the Energizer factor, which corresponds to the Agitator factor in our data from the national sample, stresses an interventive style that seems designed to increase the activity level of the family. This final factor is comprised of eight items. Two of these items (provoking and confronting) also loaded on the Agitator factor in our national sample.

Comparing the Family Therapy Models: Known-group Analysis

In this final section we shift our level of analysis from a univariate description of the attributes and practice proclivities of the known-group respondents as a whole, to an examination of similarities and differences among the trainees of Bowen, Haley, and Satir. Following the plan utilized in Chapter 3 with the national sample of family therapy practitioners, we begin with the family therapists' professional/practice experiences and activities and then move to an examination of their personality profiles. We conclude with a comparison of the belief and action systems that distinguish these three approaches to family therapy practice.

Professional/Practice Activities

Our analysis of the background data provided by the family therapists clearly indicated that the communications model's known-group respondents were an older and more experienced group than the other two known groups. The average age was 48.9 years, compared to 42.2 years for the Bowenian known group and 35.5 years for the structural/strategic known group ($p < .001$). The communications model's respondents also had significantly more prior practice experiences in working with both individuals (10.2 years, as compared to 4.4 years for the other two known groups, combined; $p < .0001$) and groups (6.2 years, as compared to 2.8 years; $p < .01$). There were no significant differences, however, among the three known groups in their respective years of family therapy practice experience, which together averaged 9.5 years. With regard to training-related professional activities, the communications model's known group again was more experienced in providing clinical supervision (6.5 years, as compared to

3.4 years for the other two combined; $p < .01$), staff development training (5.7 years, as compared to 2.4 years; $p < .005$), and in providing university instruction (3.9 years, as compared to 1.6 years; $p < .02$).

When we compared the three known groups on their *current* practice activities, however, fewer divergences were evident in the amount of time the respondents currently allotted to these same activities. More specifically, we found no significant differences when looking at the percentage of time currently devoted to individual therapy, group therapy, clinical supervision, staff development, teaching, or research activities. With regard to the provision of family therapy, however, the structural/strategic known group allotted more than half (53.7%) of their current professional activities to this area, as compared to only 26.6% for the communications known group and 33.6% for the Bowenian known group ($p < .0001$). In their actual practice of family therapy, however, the communications known group was twice as likely to involve cotherapists as the structural/strategic known group (5.5% of cases for the former, compared to 2.6% of cases for the latter; $p < .006$) and more than 10 times as likely as the Bowenian known group. On the other hand, the communications known group was significantly more likely to be providing individual therapy (20.0%, compared to 12.9% for the other two known groups combined; $p < .0001$).

When further exploring the known-group respondents' current practice activities, surprisingly, no significant differences were evidenced in their proportion of caseloads devoted to providing short-term (less than three months) treatment. When we inspected the percentage of cases seen for less than six months, however, the structural/strategic known group did exhibit statistically significant divergence from the other two family therapy models, seeing over three-fifths (61.1%) of their cases within this length time period, as compared to only approximately 40 percent for the other two models ($p < .006$). Finally, as anticipated, the Bowenian model's known group indicated that a significantly higher proportion of their current caseloads involved long-term treatment in excess of one year's duration (22.5%, as compared to 9.1% for the other two known groups combined; $p < .0003$).

When we looked at the unit of treatment utilized by these known-group practitioners, there was no significant difference in the percentage of cases involving the marital couple, averaging approximately 23.0 percent for each of the three known groups. However, this unit was the most prevalently used by the communications known group, with the whole family only slightly less prevalently used; whereas the Bowenian known group was significantly more likely to work with only the individual parent (29.8% of cases, compared to 10.7% for the other two known groups combined; $p < .0001$). On the other hand, the structural/strategic known group was significantly more likely to involve the entire family (31.1% of cases, as compared to 22.4% for the communications model's known group and only 5.6% for the Bowenian model's known group; $p < .0001$). The respondents' *preferred* units of treatment largely mirrored their current practice activities; however, for the Bowenian known group, the marital couple was rated the more preferred unit of treatment as compared to the individual parent, even though the proportion of actual current caseloads allocated to these two units of treatment was reversed. Of final interest is the fact that the representatives of all three models of family therapy worked exclusively with the children in only rare circumstances, averaging together less than 3.0 percent of their caseloads, and indicated strongly that this unit of treatment was least preferred.

Finally, when asked to describe the nature of the presenting problems seen in their current practice, we found that the communications and Bowenian known groups tended to see proportionately more cases identified as marital problems (approximately 34.1%, as compared to 21.3% for the structural/strategic group; $p < .01$), while the structural/strategic known group tended to see more cases identified as child-focused problems (40.7%, as compared to 19.3% for the other two groups combined, $p < .0001$). Not surprisingly, the respondents' *preferred* presenting problems mirrored their actual caseloads.

Table 4–3 summarizes some of the key differences in the current practice activities of the three models' known groups.

Personality Attributes (16PF)

In Table 4–4 we compare the three known groups' item means on the 16 personality factors, with *post hoc* paired comparisons that were performed to test statistically for areas of convergence and divergence. Because these 16 factors initially were constructed with varying numbers of items in each factor, the factor means presented here have been standardized to represent a possible score range of zero to 26 for each factor, with higher factor means indicating that the particular personality attribute was more descriptive of the responding group.

Our initial profile indicates that the most descriptive personality traits for the communications model's known group included the four closely related factors of Trusting, Tenderminded, Self-assured, and Venturesome (in ranked order), while Trusting, Assertive, and Self-assured were most descriptive for the structural/strategic model's

TABLE 4-3 Comparison of Known Groups on Selected Current Practice Activities.

Current Practice Activity	Theoretical Orientation			Divergence[a]
	Communications (%)	Structural/Strategic (%)	Bowenian (%)	
Proportion of current time				
Family therapy	26.58	53.73	33.60	S/S > C + B
Individual therapy	20.00	16.14	9.81	ns
Proportion of Cases Utilizing a Cotherapist	5.89	2.59	0.31	C > B
Proportion of Caseloads				
Less than 3 months	20.48	29.16	20.53	ns
3–6 months	22.26	31.95	18.20	S/S > C + B
6–12 months	17.83	15.62	18.94	ns
Over 1 year	10.70	7.54	22.49	B > C + S/S
Proportion of Caseloads				
Spouse only	12.85	8.46	29.81	B > C + S/S
Child only	4.35	3.03	0.89	S/S > B
Marital couple	25.11	22.70	23.21	ns
Whole family	22.39	31.05	5.60	S/S > C > B
Children only	2.03	3.51	0.79	ns
Proportion of Caseloads				
Marital problem	35.93	21.30	32.29	C + B > S/S
Child-focused problem	16.37	40.68	22.14	S/S > C + B
Parenting problem	11.48	7.57	7.57	ns

[a]Post hoc paired comparisons; p < .05.

TABLE 4-4 Comparison of Known Groups on Personality Factors.

Personality Factors	Theoretical Orientation			Convergence[a]	Divergence[a]
	Communications	Structural/Strategic	Bowenian		
Outgoing	14.96	14.26	14.14	C = S/S = B	None
Intelligence	13.34	14.72	14.67	S/S = B	S/S + B > C
Emotional stability	16.15	14.69	14.88	C = S/S = B	None
Assertive	16.27	16.44	14.30	C = S/S	C + S/S > B
Happy-go-lucky	14.68	13.25	11.64	C = S/S	C + S/S > B
Conscientious	12.47	12.78	13.53	C = S/S = B	None
Venturesome	16.55	13.67	12.70	S/S = B	C > S/S + B
Tenderminded	17.07	14.12	14.99	S/S = B	C > S/S + B
Trusting	17.55	17.00	17.77	C = S/S = B	None
Imaginative	14.57	13.19	13.61	C = S/S = B	None
Forthright	14.89	12.13	12.01	S/S = B	C > S/S + B
Self-assured	16.95	16.05	17.53	C = S/S C = B	B > S/S
Experimenting	14.50	13.40	14.17	C = S/S = B	None
Self-sufficient	13.20	13.98	16.90	C = S/S	B > C + S/S
Controlled	12.97	14.14	14.50	C = S/S S/S = B	B > C
Relaxed	15.95	14.74	13.95	C = S/S = B	None

[a]*Post hoc* paired comparisons; $p < .05$.

known group. For the Bowenian model's known group, Trusting and Self-assured again were the most descriptive personality attributes, followed by Self-sufficient. Hence, for all three models' known groups, the least descriptive personality attributes were Suspicious and Apprehensive, the adjective polarities for Trusting and Self-assured.

With regard to pure convergence, we found that the three models' known groups displayed statistically *nonsignificant* differences in their factor means on seven of the 16 attributes, including Outgoing, Emotional Stability, Conscientious, Trusting, Imaginative, Experimenting, and Relaxed. On the other hand, no pure divergence (statistically significant differences among each of the three groups) was evidenced. With regard to partial divergence, however, the most typical pattern was for the Bowenian known group to rate significantly lower than one or both of the other two groups on these nine remaining personality traits. This was the case in the following five partially divergent personality factors: Assertive, Happy-go-lucky, Venturesome, Tender-minded, and Forthright. On the other hand, the Bowenian known group scored above the other two known groups on Self-sufficient, joined with the structural/strategic known group in scoring higher than the communications known group on Intelligence and Controlled, and joined with the communications known group in scoring higher than the structural/strategic known group on Self-Assured.

Unlike our between-group comparisons of personality attributes of the national sample in Chapter 3, the analysis of these same attributes for the known-group respondents suggests that some rather clear associations exist between the 16PF factors and the family therapists' theoretical orientation. Indeed, nine of the 16 factors tested evidenced a statistically significant between-group difference. In addition, the patterning of these differences portrays some rather clear trends. First, what may be suggested by the data is that personality characteristics are more uniquely important to some theoretical orientations than to others. Indeed, the communications model respondents displayed pure divergence on four factors (lower on Intelligence, and higher on Venturesome, Tenderminded, and Forthright), while the Bowenian model respondents displayed pure divergence on three factors (lower on Assertive and Happy-go-lucky, and higher on Self-sufficient). On the other hand, we found that the structural/strategic model respondents did not differ statistically from the other two known groups on any of the 16 personality factors.

In addition, while Beels and Ferber's (1969) notion of a conductor/reactor personality polarity was not observed, another trend did emerge. Interestingly, for both the communications and the Bowenian models, the factors on which divergence from the other two groups was noted generally reflected outcome variables prescribed for client populations by Satir and by Bowen. The writings of Satir clearly prioritize change through the modification of family members' and therapist's ability to risk (Venturesome), to be sensitive to one another (Tenderminded), and to use congruent or "leveling" forms of communication (Forthright). Similarly, the significantly higher scores of the Bowenian respondents on the Self-sufficient, Self-assured, and Controlled factors all may reflect Bowen's emphasis on the development of autonomous or "differentiated" selves during the process of therapy.

Belief Systems (Assumption Factors)

In Table 4–5 we compare the three known groups' item means on the seven assumption factors, with *post hoc* paired comparisons performed to test statistically for areas of convergence and divergence among the three models of family therapy.

Our initial profiling indicates that the communications model's known group displayed strongest valuing of Therapist as Facilitator and Therapist as Risk-taker, while the structural/strategic model's known group valued Therapist as Director and the Bowenian model's known group valued Therapist as Theoretician. Across all three known groups, the most consistency was displayed in the high value they all placed on Family Role Structure and, perhaps surprisingly, the low value each placed on Family Responsibility.

With regard to pure convergence (statistically nonsignificant item means across all three known groups), none was evidenced. Partial convergence was evidenced in the structural/strategic and Bowenian groups' joint devaluing of Therapist as Risk-taker and Therapist as Facilitator, and in the structural/strategic and communications groups' joint devaluing of Therapist as Theoretician. As noted previously, we observed the greatest convergence for Family Role Structure, where all known-group respondents valued this factor and where the communications and Bowenian models as well as the Bowenian and structural/strategic models each joined in displaying statistically nonsignificant differences in their paired comparisons of item means.

Obviously, therefore, we can conclude that divergence was the more dominant theme in analyzing these seven assumption factors. Pure divergence occurred for the Therapist as Director, where the structural/strategic group was highest and the Bowenian group lowest; and for Family Participation, where the communications group was

TABLE 4-5 Comparison of Known Groups on Assumption Factors.

Assumption Factors[a]	Communication	Theoretical Orientation Structural/Strategic	Bowenian	Convergence[b]	Divergence[b]
Therapist as Theoretician	2.98	2.85	4.80	C = S/S	B > C + S/S
Therapist as Risk-taker	4.63	2.58	2.89	S/S = B	C > S/S + B
Therapist as Facilitator	5.34	3.57	3.54	S/S = B	C > S/S + B
Therapist as Director	3.27	4.68	2.19	None	S/S > C > B
Family Participation	3.88	3.37	2.48	None	C > S/S > B
Family Responsibility	2.47	1.28	2.26	C = B	C + B > S/S
Family Role Structure	4.54	4.89	4.19	C = S/S	S/S > B
				C = B	

[a]Factor scores represent standardized item means utilizing a scale from 1 (strongly disagree) to 6 (strongly agree).
[b]*Post hoc* paired comparisons; $p < .05$.

highest and again the Bowenian known group was lowest. Areas of partial divergence in the other five assumption factors suggest that the typical pattern was one where the communications model's known-group respondents tended to be divergently higher than one or both of the other two known groups. This was the case for Therapist as Risk-taker and Therapist as Facilitator, where the communications known group joined with the Bowenian group in evidencing item means significantly above the structural/strategic known group. On the other hand, the communications group joined with the structural/ strategic group in evidencing item means significantly below the Bowenian group on Therapist as Theoretician.

Action Systems (Style Factors)

In Table 4–6 we compare the three known groups' item means on the six style factors, again with *post hoc* paired comparisons performed to test statistically for areas of convergence and divergence among these three models of family therapy.

As was the case for the seven assumption factors, our analysis of areas of convergence displays no style factors on which pure convergence occurs. The Attender style factor appears to be the most descriptive interventive style across the three known groups, whereas no one style factor appears to be the least descriptive. For the communications model's known group, the Modeler and Attender style factors are highest, but the factors representing the remaining four interventive styles also are high, relative to the distribution of item means within the other two models' known groups. For the structural/ strategic model's known group, the Attender, Planner, and Energizer interventive styles are most descriptive, and the Analyzer least descriptive. For the Bowenian model's known group, the Attender and Composer interventive styles are most descriptive, while the Energizer is least descriptive. Finally, on none of the six style factors did the communications and the Bowenian models' known groups converge.

Obviously, once again we can conclude that divergence in style factors, as was true for the seven assumption factors, was the dominant theme. Indeed, for half of the style factors (Energizer, Analyzer, and Composer), pure divergence was evidenced. The structural/ strategic known group was significantly higher on the Energizer factor and significantly lower on the last two. Finally, with regard to partial divergence for the remaining three assumption factors, the only faint pattern was the joining of the structural/strategic and Bowenian known groups in valuing the Planner interventive style more than did

TABLE 4-6 Comparison of Known Groups on Style Factors.

Style Factors[a]	Theoretical Orientation			Convergence[b]	Divergence[b]
	Communications	Structural/Strategic	Bowenian		
Energizer	3.67	4.25	2.70	None	S/S > C > B
Attender	4.72	4.61	5.29	C = S/S	B > C + S/S
Modeler	4.85	3.83	3.63	S/S = B	C > S/S + B
Planner	3.54	4.48	4.15	S/S = B	S/S + B > C
Analyzer	3.98	2.77	3.44	None	C > B > S/S
Composer	4.12	3.59	4.50	None	B > C > S/S

[a]Factor scores represent standardized item means, utilizing a scale from 1 (not descriptive) to 6 (very descriptive).
[b]Post hoc paired comparisons; $p < .05$.

the Communications known group, and in valuing the Modeler interventive style less.

Summary

Our analysis of the data on the practice activities of known-group respondents representing each of the models of family therapy has suggested remarkably strong patterns of divergence among these models, as well as face validity with the literature. Perhaps most exemplary are the differences in the proportion of the respondents' current time devoted to family therapy as opposed to other clinical and nonclinical activities; and, more significantly, the proportion of caseloads devoted to short versus long-term treatment, as well as involving (and preferring) varying units of treatment, and definitions of the presenting problem. It was not surprising, for example, to find the Bowenian model's known-group respondents being more involved with long-term cases; or defining the unit of treatment predominantly as the adult(s); or defining the presenting problem as more typically a marital problem—particularly in contrast to the structural/strategic model's known-group respondents.

In addition, our analysis of the personality attributes of the known-group respondents reflected patterns of both convergence and uniqueness. While Trusting and Self-assured tended to be the most descriptive attributes across all three models' respondents, and Conscientious the least descriptive, we did observe a pattern whereby the communications model's respondents tended to score higher across most (over half) of the 16 personality factors. In addition, while our literature review offers few tangible clues for predicting the distinctive attributes of each model's adherents, in fact clear patterns of divergence did emerge. The Bowenian respondents tended to present a profile of detached self-assurance, scoring higher on Self-assured, Self-sufficient, and Controlled and lower on Assertive, Venturesome, and Forthright. On the other hand, the communications respondents appeared to mirror the Therapist as Risk-taker and Therapist as Facilitator assumption factors they valued, scoring higher on Venturesome, Forthright, Assertive, and Tenderminded. Interestingly, the structural/strategic model's known-group respondents reflected the most narrow range of scores across the 16 personality factors, displaying no attributes that were uniquely descriptive of this group.

When we compared the distinctive belief and action systems that emerged to represent each of the models of family therapy with the available literature in the field, the overwhelming pattern is one of isometry or congruency between this literature and each model's actual implementation by practicing family therapists intensively trained within that model. With regard to belief systems, for example, our review of the literature clearly predicted the orthogonal positions assumed by the Bowenian and structural/strategic models' known-group respondents on the Therapist as Theoretician assumption factor. Indeed, the two items loading the highest on this factor ("An extensive family history should precede family treatment" and "Family therapy should be more concerned with the past than the present") clearly validate the historical perspective and temporal orientation of the Bowenian model of family therapy.

Similarly, the communications model's valuing of Therapist as Facilitator, Therapist as Risk-taker, and Family Participation (all displaying pure divergence above the other two models' known groups) displays remarkable parallels with the typologies of family therapy models discussed in Chapter 2. These typologies portray Satir's approach as humanistic (Hansen & L'Abate, 1981), experiential (Levant, 1980), and concerned with the emotional content and meanings of communications (L'Abate & Frey, 1981). Indeed, these first two factors appear to "converge" to represent the conceptually more specific components of the Insight assumption factor discussed in Chapter 3, on which the communications model's respondents also displayed pure divergence above the other two models' representatives. In fact, of the six items comprising this Insight assumption factor created from the national survey, two items loaded on the Therapist as Risk-taker assumption factor and three on the Therapist as Facilitator assumption factor. Finally, for the structural/strategic model, the literature clearly suggests an approach to therapy where the therapist is in charge; not surprisingly, that model's known-group respondents displayed pure divergence above the other two models' on Therapist as Director, and below the other two known groups on Family Participation.

The patterning of style factors suggests a similar if not greater degree of face validity when comparisons are made with the literature in the field. The communications model's known-group respondents' strong valuing of the Modeler and Analyzer interventive styles affirms Satir's dual thrust in the therapy process: the importance of understanding the meanings and dynamics underlying human interaction, and the therapist's role in facilitating this understanding. Not surprisingly, the structural/strategic model's known-group respondents scored significantly lower on both interventive styles; indeed, the Analyzer interventive style was rated as least descriptive by that model's respondents. Finally, it also came as no surprise to find the directly orthogonal positions of the structural/strategic and Bowenian models' known groups on the Composer and Energizer interventive styles, with the former achieving pure divergence above the other two models on the Energizer interventive style, while the latter achieved pure divergence above the other two models on the Composer interventive style. The former seems to reflect the structural/strategic model's proclivity to exacerbate tensions as a way of promoting change (e.g., paradoxicals), while the latter mirrors the Bowenian model's attempt to reduce emotional overinvolvement and "reactivity," and the tension level in general, within the therapeutic process.

Overall, the findings from our known-group analysis of the three models of family therapy provide a remarkably clear panorama of the practice of family therapy and of the belief and action systems, personality attributes, and current practice activities that characterize each of the family therapy models selected for intensive investigation. Additionally, and perhaps of greater significance, we find that the known-group sampling of practitioners intensively trained by these respective models of family therapy passed the "goodness-of-fit" test with far higher marks than their "high group" national sample counterparts, both with regard to the interface of the findings with the existing literature as well as with regard to the interface of (divergent) belief and action systems *within* each family therapy model. It is toward a more intensive analysis of these two interface questions that we now turn in Chapter 5.

References

Beels, C. C. & Ferber, A. Family Therapy: A view. *Family Process*, 1969, *8*, 280–332.
Bowen, M. *Family therapy in clinical practice.* New York: Jason Aronson, 1978.
Foley, V. D. *An introduction to family therapy.* New York: Grune and Stratton, 1974.
Group for the Advancement of Psychiatry. *Treatment of families in conflict.* New York: Science House, 1970.
Gurman, A. S., & Kniskern, D. P. (Eds.). *Handbook of family therapy.* New York: Brunner/Mazel, 1981.
Hansen, J. C., & L'Abate, L. *Approaches to family therapy.* New York: Macmillan, 1981.
Hoffman, L. *Foundations of family therapy.* New York: Basic Books, 1981.
Jones, S. L. *Family therapy: A comparison of approaches.* Bowie, MD: Brady, 1980.
L'Abate, L., & Frey, J. The e-r-a model: The roles of feelings in family therapy

reconsidered: Implications for a classification of theories of family therapy. *Journal of Marital and Family Therapy*, 1981, *7*, 143–150.

Levant, R. F. A classification of the field of family therapy: A review of prior attempts and a new paradigmatic model. *American Journal of Family Therapy*, 1980, *8*, 3–16.

Madanes, C., & Haley, J. Dimensions of family therapy. *Journal of Nervous and Mental Disease*, 1977, *165*, 88–89.

Olson, D. H., Russell, C. S., & Sprenkle, D. H. Marital and family therapy: A decade review. *Journal of Marriage and the Family*, 1980, *42*, 973–994.

Watzlawick, P. J., Beavin, J. H., & Jackson, D. D. *Pragmatics of human communication*. New York: W. W. Norton, 1967.

5

Interfacing the National and Known-group Samples

In the present chapter we will compare the previous two chapters' findings pertaining to areas of convergence and divergence across the three family therapy models as derived from two data sets: the high-group respondents secured from a national survey of AAMFT and AFTA membership, and the known-group sample of graduates from the respective family therapy models' training programs. Our exploration will look at each family therapy model separately and address two interrelated questions. First, taken together, what descriptive profile do these two data sets provide concerning the belief and action systems, practice activities, and personality attributes valued and/or possessed by adherents of each particular model? Second, what are the major areas of discrepancy or disagreement in the profiles provided by these two samples; that is, in what areas do the high-group and known-group samples appear to portray each particular family therapy model in different lights?

Because each sample generated its own unique set of assumption and style factor structures, we will utilize two methods for comparing the belief and actions systems of family therapists across the two data sets for respondents oriented to each model. The first method will provide a general profile of the similarities and differences between the known-group and the high-group respondents within each model by rank-ordering the respective factor means for both groups on the assumptions and style factors generated from each data set. The second method will focus more specifically on a relative comparison of the factors themselves through the calculation of *t*-tests of the differences between these two groups' item means on each of the 12 assumption factors (seven from the known-group survey, five from the high-group survey) and each of the 12 style factors (six from the known-group survey and six from the high-group survey). Finally, after we have analyzed each model separately, we will provide a brief comparative analysis to summarize the attributes that are distinctive as well as common across all three family therapy models.

The Communications Model

The composite profile of the communications model's belief and action systems that emerged consistently portrayed a model placing strong emphasis upon the therapist's role as facilitator and risk-taker in promoting the family members' problem-solving activities. The primary goal of such activities appears to be the development of insight pertaining to the meaning and impact of varying communication patterns within the family system. To achieve these ends, family participation is valued, and the family's role structure becomes a focal point of attention. The model places a high value and emphasis on growth, which becomes a goal for family members in therapy as well as for the personal and professional development of the therapist. The therapist's intervention style in achieving these goals and processes within the therapeutic encounter is clearly and consistently one of attending, listening, analyzing, and modeling. Lesser importance is placed on interventive styles such as directing, energizing, planning, and agitating, which appear to require a higher level of activity, control, and/or directiveness on the part of the therapist.

As Table 5–1 illustrates, for example, this profile is rather consistent across the known-group and high-group respondents. Indeed, when we rank-ordered the assumption factors created solely from the *known-group* sample, the four most highly valued factors (Therapist as Facilitator, Therapist as Risk-taker, Family Role Structure, and Family Participation) were evidenced in precisely the same order as for the high-group respondents. The degree of agreement between the high-group and known-group samples was further affirmed when *t*-tests were conducted for each of these seven assumption factors. We found statistically significant differences between the known-group and high-group samples on only three of these seven factors. On two of

TABLE 5-1 Comparison of Communications Model's Known- and High-Group Respondents on Assumption and Style Factors from Known-group Survey.

Factor	(N = 49) Known Group		(N = 65) High Group		Significance Level
	$\overline{x}$	Rank	$\overline{x}$	Rank	
Assumptions					
Therapist as Facilitator	5.35	(1)	5.09	(1)	.022
Therapist as Risk-taker	4.63	(2)	4.60	(2)	ns
Family Role Structure	4.60	(3)	4.56	(3)	ns
Family Participation	3.88	(4)	3.26	(4)	.001
Therapist as Director	3.26	(5)	3.09	(6)	ns
Therapist as Theoretician	3.00	(6)	2.86	(7)	ns
Family Responsibility	2.47	(7)	3.18	(5)	.002
Styles					
Modeler	4.85	(1)	4.58	(1)	ns
Attender	4.71	(2)	4.81	(2)	ns
Composer	4.09	(3)	3.83	(4)	ns
Analyzer	3.96	(4)	4.34	(3)	.016
Energizer	3.65	(5)	3.50	(6)	ns
Planner	3.51	(6)	3.45	(5)	ns

these three factors, the known-group respondents scored higher (Therapist as Facilitator and Family Participation).

When we analyzed the six style factors created from the known-group sample, a pattern very similar to that identified for the assumption factors emerged. For all six style factors, the discrepancy in the two groups' rank ordering of these factors never exceeded one; Modeler and Attender were the two most descriptive factors for both groups, while Energizer and Planner were the two least descriptive factors. Indeed, the item means for these same four style factors were very similar when we compared the two groups' responses. This pattern of similarity in the responses perhaps is emphasized most dramatically in the *t*-tests for the style factors, where we found statistically significant differences on only one (Analyzer) of these six factors.

When we consider the factors generated solely from the high-group sample, shown in Table 5–2, once again we find that agreement across these two groups is the rule. For both groups, the two most highly valued assumption factors were Insight and Professional

TABLE 5-2 Comparison of Communication Model's Known- and High-group Respondents on Assumption and Style Factors from High-group Survey.

	(N = 49) Known Group		(N = 65) High Group		
Factor	$\bar{x}$	Rank	$\bar{x}$	Rank	Significance Level
Assumptions					
Professional Growth	5.16	(1)	4.81	(2)	.008
Insight	5.09	(2)	5.05	(1)	ns
Problem Solving	4.30	(3)	4.26	(3)	ns
A-traditionalism	3.43	(4)	3.95	(4)	.004
Systemic View	3.30	(5)	2.67	(5)	.001
Styles					
Attender	4.82	(1)	4.85	(1)	ns
Modeler	4.59	(2)	4.35	(2)	ns
Detoxifier	4.18	(3)	3.75	(4)	.044
Director	3.93	(4)	3.60	(5)	.043
Prober	3.68	(5)	4.06	(3)	.014
Agitator	3.31	(6)	3.28	(6)	ns

Growth, with the latter being most strongly valued by the known group. On the other hand, the two least valued assumption factors were Systemic View and A-traditionalism. Furthermore, for both samples the Attender and Modeler interventive styles were rated as being most descriptive of their practice, while the Agitator style was rated as being least descriptive. The statistically significant shifts occurred in the known group's stronger valuing of the Detoxifier and the Director interventive styles and its lesser valuing of the Prober interventive style.

When we turn to the underlying personality attributes of adherents to the communications model (not shown in the table), once again strong agreement between the two data sets is the rule. Both the high-group and the known-group samples ranked Trusting, Tender-minded, Self-assured, and Emotional Stability as four of the five most descriptive attributes. Interestingly, we found somewhat less agreement among the least descriptive attributes, although, perhaps surprisingly, both samples rated Conscientious and Self-sufficient as two of the three least descriptive personality attributes. A general overview of the personality factors' means suggests a trend for the known-group respondents to score higher than their high-group counterparts across all of these 16 factors. Indeed, we found statistically significant differences in favor of higher scores for the known-group respondents for the following four personality attributes: Venturesome ($p < .032$), Happy-go-lucky ($p < .002$), Assertive ($p < .002$), and Experimenting ($p < .002$).

Finally, when we looked at the nature of the communications model's respondents' prior experience and current practice activities, some interesting patterns emerged. With regard to prior experience, the known-group sample had more practice experience in family therapy, while the high-group sample had more experience in individual therapy. However, the known group's greater amount of overall experience was most evident in such training formats as clinical supervision, staff development, and teaching. This same pattern, however, was not as clearly evident when profiling the two samples' *current* professional activities. Indeed, we found that the communications model's high-group respondents were devoting almost twice as much of their current professional activities to the same training-related (or nonclinical) activities as the known group, while the known-group sample was almost twice as heavily involved in providing family therapy. In summary, the known-group respondents appear to have narrowed the range of their professional activities toward a more concentrated focus on doing family therapy, whereas the high-group respondents appear to be moving in the opposite direction.

A more intensive inspection of the communications model's respondents' current practice activities indicated strong agreement between the two samples in their utilizing shorter-term treatment (of six months' duration or less); however, the high group showed a marked tendency to move toward a more structured and time-limited treatment modality (less than three months' duration), as compared to the known-group sample. With regard to the respondents' preferred unit of treatment, the known group rated the family as a whole more strongly and the marital couple second, while the high group sample reversed this order. While both groups rated the three other units of treatment (adult/spouse only, child only, and all children only) as all representing very low priorities, their actual proportion of current caseloads involving these three low-rated units showed a clear preference in both samples for working with the adult/spouse only. Not surprisingly, the known group's predominant unit of treatment in their actual current caseloads was the whole family (reflecting their preferred unit), while the high group's predominant unit was the marital couple. The disparity between these actual proportions of current caseloads, however, was insignificant for the known group but showed a ratio of 3 to 1 (marital couple versus whole family) for the high group. Finally, no differences were evidenced when we looked at the presenting problems in the two groups' caseloads. Marital problems were most strongly preferred by both, while child-focused problems were least preferred; and the proportions of caseloads comprised of each of these identified problem areas, not surprisingly, mirrored both groups' stated preferences.

The Structural/Strategic Model

Unlike the communications model, a composite profile of the structural/strategic model's belief and action systems as derived from a comparison of the high-group and known-group samples does not readily emerge.

Beginning, therefore, with the belief systems of only the *known-group* structural/strategic sample, the profile of the therapeutic process

TABLE 5–3 Comparison of Structural/Strategic Model's Known- and High-group Respondents on Assumption and Style Factors from Known-group Survey.

Factor	(N = 37) Known Group		(N = 42) High Group		Significance Level
	$\overline{x}$	Rank	$\overline{x}$	Rank	
Assumptions					
Family Role Structure	4.97	(1)	4.84	(1)	ns
Therapist as Director	4.75	(2)	3.64	(4)	.001
Therapist as Facilitator	3.65	(3)	4.42	(2)	.002
Family Participation	3.46	(4)	3.63	(5)	ns
Therapist as Theoretician	2.87	(5)	2.75	(6)	ns
Therapist as Risk-taker	2.60	(6)	3.91	(3)	.001
Family Responsibility	1.26	(7)	2.61	(7)	.001
Styles					
Attender	4.67	(1)	4.31	(1)	.024
Planner	4.44	(2)	3.39	(4)	.001
Energizer	4.22	(3)	3.39	(4)	.001
Modeler	3.83	(4)	4.24	(2)	.029
Composer	3.50	(5)	3.72	(3)	ns
Analyzer	2.69	(6)	3.50	(6)	.001

TABLE 5–4 Comparison of Structural/Strategic Model's Known- and High-group Respondents on Assumption and Style Factors from High-group Survey.

Factor	(N = 37) Known Group		(N = 42) High Group		Significance Level
	$\overline{x}$	Rank	$\overline{x}$	Rank	
Assumptions					
A-traditionalism	5.40	(1)	4.44	(1)	.001
Problem Solving	4.19	(2)	3.98	(4)	ns
Insight	2.92	(3)	4.19	(2)	.001
Systemic View	2.86	(4)	2.89	(5)	ns
Professional Growth	2.46	(5)	4.02	(3)	.001
Styles					
Director	4.65	(1)	3.66	(4)	.001
Attender	4.26	(2)	4.26	(1)	ns
Modeler	3.86	(3)	3.97	(2)	ns
Detoxifier	3.82	(4)	3.67	(3)	ns
Agitator	3.69	(5)	3.21	(6)	.047
Prober	3.21	(6)	3.42	(5)	ns

portrayed in Tables 5–3 and 5–4 suggests that the focal point of therapy is the family role structure and that the process of therapy requires a more directive stance on the part of the therapist, with a concomitant strong de-emphasis on family responsibility and (to a lesser degree) family participation. Problem-solving activities, as well as a-traditional approaches to the treatment process, become important, while the role of insight and history or past events, as well as the professional growth of the practitioner, are all devalued.

The profile of the structural/strategic model's belief system as portrayed by the high-group sample also supports the importance of a-traditional approaches to the therapeutic process but more strongly affirms the value of insight and the professional growth of the practitioner. Indeed, the discrepancies between these two groups' belief systems become most evident when we compare their responses on the assumption factors created by the *known group* survey (Table 5–3). Although the Family Role Structure factor was ranked the highest and the Family Responsibility factor the lowest for both groups, they differed with regard to their ranking of all five of the remaining assumption factors. The high group assumed a less directive stance by ranking the Therapist as Facilitator factor second and the Therapist as Risk-taker factor third, while ranking the Therapist as Director fourth. On the other hand, the known-group respondents affirmed the "therapist in control" stance, as evidenced by their ranking of the Therapist as Director factor second. Furthermore, it appears that the distribution of item means suggests that the known group assumes a more polarized view of practice, since their top two assumption factors are more strongly valued than the high group's top two and their two least valued ones are more strongly devalued. Finally, the diversity of the profiles suggested by the two different samples is evidenced further by the significant statistical differences in the means for four of these seven assumption factors.

Similarly, when the two samples' belief systems were compared on the five assumption factors created by the *high-group* survey (Table 5–4), we once again can observe marked discrepancies with regard to both the rank order of preference and the between-group *t*-tests. The most prominent discrepancies in the comparison of the rank ordering of factors emerged for the Problem Solving and Professional Growth factors, the former ranked higher by the known-group respondents, while the latter ranked lower. Reflected also by the rank-order procedure, but more striking in the between-group tests of factor means, was the known group's stronger devaluing of the Insight and Professional Growth assumption factors, as well as its stronger valuing of the A-traditionalism factor. Once again we also can observe the same polarization trend noted previously among the known-group respondents.

We now turn to the profiles of the action systems of the known- and high-group respondents, as suggested by Tables 5–3 and 5–4. Beginning first with the *known-group* respondents, we see that the therapeutic role places emphasis upon listening and information retrieval skills (e.g., Attender), while also stressing the therapist's responsibility for the conduct of therapy through purposeful and goal-directed therapeutic activities (e.g., Director, Planner). A clear de-emphasis upon therapeutic activities directed toward assessing the dynamics underlying interpersonal behavior (e.g., Analyzer, Prober) also characterizes the profile suggested by these known-group respondents.

The profile of the interventive styles of the structural/strategic model's *high-group* respondents both parallels and diverges from that suggested by their known-group counterparts. While the listening and information-retrieval skills also are emphasized in the style profile for these high-group respondents, they tended to place less of a priority on the more active, therapist-in-control factors (e.g., Planner, Energizer, Agitator), while assigning a higher priority to the role of therapeutic modeling in their overall interventive repertoire.

Examining the factor rankings for each group first, Table 5–3 indicates that both groups ranked the Attender and Analyzer first and last, respectively; while the Modeler and Composer factors were more highly valued (ranked second and third) by the high group than by the known group (ranked fourth and fifth). Once again, the same polarization process also is evidenced by the known-group respondents. When we consider the statistical tests of the differences between factor means, the discrepant findings are highlighted even more. Indeed, as we can observe in Table 5–3, the two samples' factor means were significantly different for five of the six style factors. The known-group respondents scored significantly higher than the high-group respondents on the Attender, Planner, and Energizer style factors and significantly lower on the Modeler and Analyzer factors.

On the other hand, when comparing these two groups on the style factors created by the *high-group* survey (Table 5–4), we observed fewer discrepancies with regard to the rank ordering and the between-group *t*-tests. Clearly the major difference in the rank ordering was in regard to the Director factor, ranked first by the known-group and fourth by the high-group respondents. This also is reflected in the between-sample tests ($p < .001$). The only other style factor for which a significant difference was observed was Agitator, wherein the known-group respondents also scored higher.

When we turn to the personality attributes of the adherents to the structural/strategic model, the profiles of the high- and known-group samples were remarkably similar. Indeed, only on two personality factors, Emotional Stability ($p < .015$) and Self-assured ($p < .001$), were statistically significant differences evidenced; in both instances, the known-group respondents scored significantly lower. Overall, four of the five most descriptive attributes for both samples were the following: Trusting, Self-assured, Emotional Stability, and Relaxed; while two of the three least descriptive personality attributes for both were Conscientious and Happy-go-lucky.

When we looked at the structural/strategic model's respondents' prior experiences and current practice activities, some interesting patterns of similarity and differences between the two groups emerged. With regard to prior experience, the known-group sample actually was a younger group and had more years of family therapy experience but fewer years of individual therapy experience when compared to the high-group sample. The major differentiating area was in nonclinical-related prior experiences, where the high-group respondents averaged more years of such training activities as clinical supervision, staff development, and teaching. This same patterning was even more pronounced when we assessed the respondents' current practice activities. Here, the structural/strategic model's high-group sample spent almost three times as much of their current time providing such training activities. On the other hand, the known-group respondents spent more than half of their time (56.1%) providing family therapy, as compared to approximately only one-third (36.0%) for the high-group sample. At the same time, however, the known-group respondents devoted considerably less time to individual therapy. In summary, the known-group respondents appear to reflect a consistent focus on doing family therapy (both past and present), whereas the high-group respondents appear to be pursuing more diverse professional activities, perhaps with even greater vigor in the present.

Our inspection of the nature of the two groups' current practice activities indicated that both were unlikely to practice family therapy with cotherapists but that the known group was approximately three times less likely to do so, utilizing cotherapists in less than 3 percent of their cases. With regard to the average length of their cases, approximately three-fifths of both the high-group and known-group respondents' cases were six months in duration or shorter. Surprisingly, however, the high group indicated a slightly stronger preference for a shorter-term (less than three months) treatment modality.

With regard to the respondents' preferred unit of treatment, both rated the whole family as the most preferred and the marital couple second; however, there was a more marked disparity between these two rankings for the known-group respondents. This disparity was played out even more markedly when we looked at their actual caseloads. For the known group, the most predominant unit of treatment was the entire family (31.1% of cases), followed by the marital couple (22.7% of cases); whereas for the high group the figures basically were reversed (32.7% of cases involved the marital couple as the unit of treatment, while only 23.8% of cases involved the entire family). The other three units of treatment (adult/spouse only, child only, all children only) were rated very low in preference by both groups. Finally, with regard to the presenting problem, we found that the known-group respondents indicated strongest preference for working with child-focused problems. Not surprisingly, they also indicated that the largest proportion of their current caseloads were so defined. The high-group respondents most strongly preferred marital problems, also not surprising in light of the previous findings indicating that the largest proportion of their current caseload was the marital couple.

The Bowenian Model

As an inspection of Tables 5-5 and 5-6 suggests, the development of a composite profile of the belief and action systems of the Bowenian model for respondents from both samples proved to be an even more tenuous and uncertain task than that posed by the structural/strategic model. Consequently, as in the case of the structural/strategic model, we will review the profiles suggested by the two groups separately for both belief and action systems.

Beginning first with the belief systems (assumption factors) of only the *known-group* sample, we find that these respondents are most clearly characterized by their use of a systemic view of dysfunctioning that emphasizes the role of family history in defining current interaction, as well as their adherence to a group of nontraditional family practice beliefs. The role structure of the family is an important target of their interventions, and they tend to see a strong correlation between therapeutic effectiveness and their own personal growth. On the other hand, these known-group respondents tend to de-emphasize the therapist's promotion of the client's learning through insight, while at the

TABLE 5-5 Comparison of Bowenian Model's Known- and High-group Respondents on Assumption and Style Factors from Known-group Survey.

Factor	(N = 70) Known Group		(N = 36) High Group		Significance Level
	$\overline{x}$	Rank	$\overline{x}$	Rank	
Assumptions					
Therapist as Theoretician	4.80	(1)	3.46	(4)	.001
Family Role Structure	4.24	(2)	4.75	(1)	.019
Therapist as Facilitator	3.60	(3)	4.75	(1)	.001
Therapist as Risk-taker	2.90	(4)	4.17	(3)	.001
Family Participation	2.51	(5)	3.35	(5)	.001
Family Responsibility	2.26	(6)	3.13	(7)	.001
Therapist as Director	2.21	(7)	3.29	(6)	.001
Styles					
Attender	5.29	(1)	4.88	(1)	.007
Composer	4.50	(2)	3.81	(4)	.001
Planner	4.12	(3)	3.47	(5)	.002
Modeler	3.63	(4)	3.99	(3)	.050
Analyzer	3.41	(5)	4.05	(2)	.005
Energizer	2.67	(6)	3.21	(6)	.001

TABLE 5-6 Comparison of Bowenian Model's Known- and High-group Respondents on Assumption and Style Factors from High-group Survey.

Factor	(N = 70) Known Group		(N = 36) High Group		Significance Level
	$\overline{x}$	Rank	$\overline{x}$	Rank	
Assumptions					
A-traditionalism	4.76	(1)	4.01	(3)	.001
Professional Growth	4.04	(2)	4.51	(2)	.001
Problem Solving	3.87	(3)	3.87	(4)	ns
Systemic View	3.63	(4)	3.18	(5)	.007
Insight	3.24	(5)	4.65	(1)	.001
Styles					
Attender	4.79	(1)	4.65	(1)	ns
Director	3.87	(2)	3.40	(5)	.004
Prober	3.85	(3)	4.02	(2)	ns
Detoxifier	3.84	(4)	3.63	(4)	ns
Modeler	3.47	(5)	3.95	(3)	.012
Agitator	2.31	(6)	2.95	(6)	.001

same time they reflect the apparent paradoxical positions (first noted in Chapter 3) of minimizing family participation while at the same time also minimizing the therapist's responsibility for directing the conduct of therapy.

The *high-group* Bowenians, on the other hand, project a belief system that clearly is more concerned with the role of insight in the change process and somewhat less wedded to the use of the past and family history as avenues for change. Rather, they tend to focus more on the role structure of the family and make greater use of the more traditional therapeutic reality-testing and facilitating techniques, to achieve more effective and satisfying patterns of intrafamily communication.

When we compared the Bowenian model's high and known groups' responses on the seven assumption factors derived from the *known-group* survey (Table 5–5), some rather similarly valued clusters of assumptions emerged. In particular, Family Participation, Family Responsibility, and Therapist as Director occupy the lowest three rankings for both the known and high groups, while Therapist as Theoretician, Family Role Structure, Therapist as Facilitator, and Therapist as Risk-taker occupy the top four ranks across the samples. Yet the contrast in regard to the valuing of the Therapist as Theoretician (ranked first in the known-group sample and fourth in the high-group sample), and the consistent finding of significant *t*-test differences between group means for *each* of the seven assumption factors, tends to override these similarities observed through the rank-ordering procedure. With regard to the direction of the discrepancies suggested by these seven assumption factors, it is worth noting that the known-group respondents had significantly lower factor means than did the high-group respondents for six of the seven assumption factors. Not surprisingly, only on the Therapist as Theoretician factor, comprised by items that strongly reflect the writings of Murray Bowen and his associates, did the known-group respondents score significantly higher than their high-group counterparts.

When we compare the five assumption factors created from the *high-group* survey (Table 5–6), the findings are similar. As in the case of the known-group survey's factors, the rank-order discrepancy for one particular factor seemed rather accentuated; the Insight factor was ranked first by the high-group sample and last by the known-group sample. Similarly, following the pattern we found in Table 5–5, significant differences between group means emerged for four of the five high-group assumption factors. Unlike the previous comparisons, however, no pattern of directionality emerged. The high-group respondents were significantly higher than the known-group respondents on two factors (Insight and Professional Growth), while the known-group respondents also displayed significantly higher item means for two factors (A-traditionalism and Systemic View). Overall, when looking at both sets of assumption factors, we also do not find the same marked polarization in belief systems among the Bowenian model's known group as was characteristic of the structural/strategic model's known group.

When we examine the profiles of the interventive styles from Tables 5–5 and 5–6, once again similarities and differences can be observed between the Bowenian model's two groups. Looking first at the profile of the *known-group* respondents, the tables suggest an action system characterized by primary adherence to therapeutic "attending" skills that emphasize the role of responding to client feelings and behavior as well as stressing the therapist's function in information retrieval. The more "active" therapeutic roles (e.g., Agitator, Energizer) are de-emphasized, particularly those that stress the therapist's role in disequilibrating the family system and in increasing its activity level, while the less active ones are stressed (e.g., Detoxifier, Composer).

Similarly, while the profile of the *high-group* respondents also reflects this same emphasis on the less "active" interventive styles, clear differences between the two groups also are suggested. In particular, the profile for the high-group respondents suggests less willingness to incorporate the therapist-in-control style factors (e.g., Planner, Director) into their treatment repertoire, while engaging more in interpretive and modeling activities (e.g., Analyzer, Modeler). Yet, at the same time they also display more willingness to heighten the activity level of the therapeutic process (e.g., Energizer, Agitator).

When we compare the two Bowenian groups first on the six style factors created from the *known-group* survey (Table 5–5), the Attender and Energizer are ranked first and last, respectively, in both data sets. However, the rank ordering of the Analyzer is particularly discrepant (fifth in the known-group responses, second in the high group). Perhaps even more dramatically, as in the case of the assumption factors, significant between-group differences emerged for the *t*-tests on *each* of these six known-group style factors. The known-group respondents were significantly higher on the Attender, Composer, and Planner interventive styles, while the high group's endorsement of the more active Modeler, Analyzer, and Energizer interventive styles was significantly higher than that of the known group.

Finally, when we compare the two groups on the six style factors created from the *high-group* survey (Table 5–6), the between-sample discrepancies, while apparent, were not as evident as in all previous comparisons. Indeed, although the Director was ranked second in the known-group sample and fifth in the high-group sample, three of the six style factors were ranked in exactly the same manner. The Attender interventive style was ranked first, the Agitator last, and the Detoxifier fourth for both groups. More dramatically, no statistical differences were observed between groups for half of the factors (Attender, Prober, and Detoxifier). With regard to the remaining three factors, the known-group respondents had significantly higher factor means for the Director style, and significantly lower scores for the Modeler and the Agitator style factors. Comparing both sets of data, however, we do find a polarization process among the known-group respondents' interventive styles that was not evident when looking at their belief systems.

When we profile the personality attributes of the Bowenian model's high- and known-group samples, we find that both groups rated Trusting and Self-assured as the two most descriptive personality attributes, and they agreed on four of the five least descriptive attributes, including Happy-go-lucky, Forthright, Conscientious, and Imaginative. The only statistically significant difference between these two groups was evidenced for the Venturesome personality factor, where the high group's factor mean ranked this attribute fifth *most* descriptive, while the known ⁓roup's factor mean ranked it as the third *least* descriptive attribute ($p < .002$). Perhaps of final interest is the fact that the differences in the Bowenian model's high- and known-group samples' scores on the Self-sufficient personality factor approached statistical significance, being ranked third most descriptive for the known group but only seventh most descriptive for the high group ($p < .06$).

Finally, when we look at the nature of the Bowenian model's respondents' prior experiences and current practice activities, we find that, while both samples averaged the same age, surprisingly the high-group sample was the more experienced one—not simply in their years of clinical practice working with families, individuals, and groups, but also in their years of training-related activities such as clinical supervision, staff development, and teaching. With regard to their *current* practice activities, however, the known-group sample spent more of their time providing family therapy (43.0%, compared to 33.0%), while the high group spent over three times as much of their time providing individual therapy. Finally, in providing family therapy these groups differed markedly in their tendency to use cotherapists, with the high group using cotherapists in almost 9 percent of their cases, which was almost 3 times more likely than the known group.

A more intensive analysis of the respondents' current practice activities depicted general patterns of similarity as well as dissimilarity between the two groups. With regard to the length of their cases, for example, we found that both groups were likely to involve up to half of their current caseloads in longer-term (over six months) treatment and to involve approximately only one-fifth of their cases in short-term treatment (under three months). On the other hand, while both groups indicated that their preferred unit of treatment was the marital couple, the known group's next most preferred unit was the adult/spouse while the high group's was the entire family. This discrepancy was even more evident when we looked at the respondents' caseloads, where the adult/spouse was the predominant unit of treatment for the known-group sample. Not surprisingly, both groups indicated strong preferences for working with marital problems and indicated that this represented the predominant presenting problem in their caseloads. Clearly the pattern of current practice activities for both groups of Bowenian adherents reflected longer-term treatment directed toward the marital couple and/or adult client.

Comparing the Three Family Therapy Models

Having examined each model of family therapy separately across its respective high- and known-group samples, in this section we will shift to a comparative view of the three models by highlighting the similarities and unique properties that emerged from this cross-sample perspective. We begin this discussion with an examination of belief and action systems and conclude it with a survey of personality attributes and practice activities.

Belief and Action Systems

As the separate analyses of each model have suggested, we observed both similarities and differences with regard to belief and action systems as we moved from the inspection of high-group to known-group assumption and style factor scores. With regard to these differences, while substantial shifts in the characterization of family therapy practice were observed between high- and known-groups for each model, the pervasiveness of these shifts is dramatically different. Clearly, we can observe a continuum across the three models, beginning with the communications model at one extreme, where the known group was significantly different from the high group on less than half of the assumption and style factors tested (10 of 24); and ranging to the opposite extreme with the Bowenian model, where between-group differences remarkably emerged for 20 of the 24 assumption and style factors tested. The structural/strategic model positioned itself at a point between the two extremes, with significant between-group differences on 14 of the 24 assumption and style factors generated from the known- and high-group studies. We also might note that the changes observed did not favor either belief or action system for any of the three models. For the communications model, six of the 10 changes (significant differences) observed were for assumption factors and four for style factors; for the structural/strategic model, seven of the 14 factors were assumption factors and seven were style factors; and, finally, for the Bowenian model, 11 of the 20 factors for which significant differences were observed were assumption factors and nine were style factors.

In Table 5–7 we summarize the nature of the outcomes for each model when the scores of the high-group respondents were compared with those of the known-group respondents for each of the 12 assumption factors. The symbol "0" (zero) indicates that both groups' factor means were not statistically different for a particular factor. The symbol "+" indicates that the known-group scores were significantly higher,

TABLE 5-7 Comparison of the Three Models: Changes in Assumption Factors from High to Known Groups.

	Model[a]		
Assumption Factors	*Communications*	*Structural/ Strategic*	*Bowenian*
Known-group Factors			
Therapist as Theoretician	0	0	+
Therapist as Risk-taker	0	-	-
Therapist as Facilitator	+	-	-
Therapist as Director	0	+	-
Family Participation	+	0	-
Family Responsibility	-	-	-
Family Role Structure	0	0	-
High-group Factors			
Insight	0	-	-
Professional Growth	+	-	-
Systemic View	+	0	+
Problem Solving	0	0	0
A-traditionalism	-	+	+

[a]The symbol "0" (zero) indicates that statistically insignificant differences ($p < .05$) emerged from the comparison of assumption factor means between high-group and known-group respondents; the symbol "+" indicates that known-group scores were significantly higher; and the symbol "-" indicates that known-group scores were significantly lower than the high group's.

while the symbol "$-$" indicates that the known-group scores were significantly lower than the high-group scores. As the table suggests, similar outcomes for the assumption factor means resulted for all three models only in the case of two of the 12 factors: Family Responsibility and Problem Solving. For the Family Responsibility factor, the movement from high- to known-group was characterized by significantly lower scores for known-group representatives of each of the three models; for the Problem-Solving factor, significant between-group differences were not observed for any of the models. The most powerful convergent pattern that emerged among these assumption factors, however, was the similarity between the structural/strategic and Bowenian models. Rather remarkably, as depicted in Table 5–7, similar outcomes were evidenced for these two models on seven of the 12 assumption factors. Interestingly, these shifts collectively suggest that both structural/strategic and Bowenian known-group respondents placed *less* value on a cluster of factors associated with more traditional aspects of the therapeutic role (Therapist as Risk-taker, Therapist as

TABLE 5-8 Comparison of the Three Models: Changes in Style Factors from High to Known Groups.

	Model[a]		
Style Factors	*Communications*	*Structural/ Strategic*	*Bowenian*
Known-group Factors			
Energizer	0	+	–
Attender	0	+	+
Modeler	0	–	–
Planner	0	+	+
Analyzer	–	–	–
Composer	0	0	+
High-group Factors			
Attender	0	0	0
Director	+	+	+
Agitator	0	+	–
Prober	–	0	0
Modeler	0	0	–
Detoxifier	+	0	0

[a]The symbol "0" (zero) indicates that statistically insignificant differences ($p < .05$) emerged from the comparison of assumption factor scores between high-group and known-group respondents; the symbol "+" indicates that known-group scores were significantly higher; the symbol "–" indicates that known-group scores were significantly lower than the high group's.

Facilitator, Family Responsibility, Insight, and Professional Growth), while placing more value on a single factor reflecting a group of out-of-the-mainstream therapeutic ideas (A-traditionalism).

In Table 5-8 we summarize the similarities among the three models that emerged from an examination of the 12 interventive style factors. As in the case of the assumption factors, only two style factors were identified on which the statistical tests of the means between the high- and the known-group respondents produced similar outcomes for all three models. On one of these factors (Analyzer), factor means for all three family therapy models were significantly lower for the known-group respondents than for their high-group counterparts. Conversely, for the Attender (high-group factor), no significant differences were observed in the factor means for the known and high groups across all three models. Beyond these convergent factors, and in a manner strikingly parallel to the findings reported previously for the assumption factors, we find that the major pattern to emerge from the data was the congruency between the structural/strategic and

Bowenian models. Again, the convergence between respondents representing these models and their consequent divergence from the communications model's respondents is striking. Indeed, on two-thirds of the style factors tested (eight out of 12), we observed congruent patterns between structural/strategic and Bowenian respondents. On three factors, the known-group respondents for both models scored significantly higher (Attender, Planner, and Director), while on two additional factors the scores for the known-group respondents for both models were significantly lower (Modeler and Analyzer). These two patterns may suggest a tendency among known-group respondents for both of these models to place a greater emphasis on the therapist-in-control interventive styles and less emphasis on those styles promoting education, insight, and awareness. These findings appear to reinforce the finding of significantly higher scores on the A-traditionalism assumption factor by the known-group adherents of both models, as previously discussed in Table 5–7.

Personality Attributes and Practice Activities

When we turn to a comparison of the three family therapy models' respondents' personality attributes, we find that Trusting, Self-assured, and Emotional Stability consistently were rated as three of the five most descriptive attributes. Hence, their polar opposites of Suspicious, Apprehensive, and Affected by Feelings (respectively) were the least descriptive ones. The communications model's respondents, however, did tend to rate Outgoing and Tenderminded higher, and Self-sufficient lower, while the structural/strategic model's respondents indicated that Assertive was a more descriptive personality attribute. Finally, the Bowenian model's respondents scored notably higher than the other two models' respondents on Self-sufficient and, to a lesser degree, on Controlled and Conscientious. On the other hand, they rated Outgoing as less descriptive, and joined with the structural/strategic model's respondents in also rating Forthright and Tenderminded as less descriptive.

When we inspect the three family therapy models' respondents' prior experience, we find that the structural/strategic model's adherents were the youngest and least experienced in their range of clinical and nonclinical (supervising, teaching, and staff development) activities, while the communications model's respondents were the oldest and most experienced. Interestingly, and as noted previously in this chapter, we found that the within-group analysis indicated a relative *decline* in age, as well as in the clinical and nonclinical work experience activities, when moving from the high-group to the known-group samples for both the Bowenian and structural/strategic models' respondents, while the opposite trend is in evidence for the communications model's respondents—particularly in the communications model's known group being older and having had more years of nonclinical work experience.

With regard to the respondents' current clinical practice, all three *known-group* samples were utilizing family therapy as the predominant mode of treatment, with the structural/strategic known group highest (spending over one-half of their current practice time in this activity). For the communications and Bowenian *high groups*, however, providing individual therapy consumed the more significant proportion of their current clinical practice (averaging over one-third of each group's time). We might note, however, that as one moves from the high-group to the known-group samples, the percentage of current practice time devoted to family therapy increases in roughly the same proportion for all three family therapy models, while the proportion of time devoted to individual therapy declines for all three models, most dramatically for the Bowenian model and least so for the communications model. Of final interest is the fact that the use of cotherapists in the respondents' provision of family therapy was relatively minimal across all three models (the Bowenian model's high-group sample rated the highest, utilizing cotherapists in only approximately 8.0 percent of their cases), and this usage declined when moving from high-group to known-group samples within each of these three family therapy models, most particularly for the Bowenian and structural/strategic models.

When we compare the three models of family therapy on the duration of their cases, we find clear differences among the models but relatively similar profiles when comparing the high- and known-group samples within each model. Unquestionably, the structural/strategic respondents more frequently utilized short-term treatment (approximately 70.0% of both the high-group and known-group samples' cases were six months or less), while the Bowenian respondents utilized it least (in approximately 40.0% of both its high-group and known-group samples' cases). On the other hand, we found that almost one-fourth of the Bowenian model's cases were seen for at least one year, which happened in only about one-tenth of the cases for both the structural/strategic and the communications models' high- and known-group samples.

In looking at the respondents' preferred units of treatment, clear differences again emerged. The Bowenian model's high- and known-group samples placed strongest preference for working with the marital couple; however, the known group rated the adult/spouse (only) as a much more strongly preferred unit than did its high-group counterpart. The structural/strategic model's two groups, on the other hand, indicated strongest preference for working with the family unit as a whole, with the marital couple second (with the known group displaying the stronger preference for the whole family as the unit of treatment). For the communications model, however, the high-group sample indicated strongest preference for working with the marital couple (with the family unit being second), but reversed this order for its known-group counterpart. The structural/strategic and communications models' high- and known-group samples indicated a markedly lesser valuing for working with the adult/spouse (only) as compared to both Bowenian groups' responses. Not surprisingly, the respondents' actual caseloads reflected these preferences. For the Bowenian model's two groups, the most notable decline in moving from the high-group sample to the known-group sample was found in the percentage of caseloads involving the whole family as the unit of treatment. On the other hand, this figure actually increased (and the proportion of cases involving the marital couple decreased) when moving from the high-group to the known-group samples for both the structural/strategic and the communications models' respondents.

Summary and Conclusions

Our within-model comparisons of respondents comprising the high groups and known groups of the three models of family therapy are highlighted by three major trends in the data. First, in response to the question of whether the practice dimensions and preferences differ between known- and high-group representatives of the same model, our data have suggested that the answer to this question is generally no or at best equivocal for one model (communications), generally yes for a second model (structural/strategic), and emphatically yes for the third model (Bowenian). Second, and in response to the question of whether the shift from high to known group would impact therapeutic belief and action systems differentially, the answer is clearly no. No composite trend was observed for any model. Finally, in response to the question of whether or not the movement from high to known group suggested patterns of similarity between models, the answer is emphatically yes. Known-group respondents representing the structural/strategic and Bowenian groups differed from their high-group counterparts in a remarkably similar fashion.

While these three trends are readily discernible, explanations for these findings must be pursued with sincere caution. Our findings do in fact affirm the impact or influence of intensive training or exposure to family therapy practice, particularly for the Bowenian and structural/strategic models' adherents. In both cases their known-group respondents expressed significantly different belief and action systems than their high-group counterparts. In both cases, their known-group respondents also displayed a polarization process in their belief and action systems, tending to be significantly stronger in their valuing of the highest rated factors and significantly lower in their rating of the lowest rated factors. Finally, in both cases, their known-group respondents' belief and action systems (and practice activities) tended to be more congruent with the theoretical underpinnings of that particular model, as reflected by the family therapy literature.

Obviously, one interpretation might be that it is easier to develop one's clinical repertoire from the literature on the communications model, whereas the other two models may require a more intensive socialization process involving the experiential and role modeling activities of formal training programs. A second but perhaps related interpretation might be that Satir's actual training activities and workshops (in general) have already reached and had their impact on a far wider national audience. Hence the distinction between a national sample (high group) and members of her selective Avanta Network Training program (known group) may be a less meaningful or discriminating one for the communications model of family therapy.

Finally, it may be that the same "conversion process" discussed in Chapter 3 also might help to explain these findings. In the national sample we found strong evidence that certain belief and action systems that had their roots in traditional, psychodynamically oriented individual therapy indeed were alive and well among our responding family therapists. At the same time we suggested a "cultural lag process" also might be operating in these findings, wherein some of the more "a-traditional" elements of practice espoused by the family therapy movement were yet to take hold among this national sample. It is arguable, then, that the communications model more strongly shares these more traditional value systems about the therapeutic enterprise; therefore, those on the national scene who might be less actively involved in pursuing intensive professional development opportunities *in family therapy* might view the communications model's more traditional value system as representing an easier and/or more compatible transition to make along this path of professional development as a family therapist.

While other explanations perhaps are available, we believe that the most essential finding from our analyses should not be lost: There is a socialization process that in fact does take place as a result of intensive training in a particular model of family therapy. This process, in turn, does increase the degree of congruency between what the pioneers/exemplars and theoreticians of a model write about and what subsequent generations of family therapists actually advocate as the goals and processes of their therapeutic endeavors. In Chapter 6, therefore, we will explore the literature on the training and supervision of family therapists, in an effort to understand further the mechanisms by which the impact of this socialization process might be promoted.

6

The Supervision and Training of Family Therapists[1]

In our analysis and discussion of the three family therapy models, we found a clear pattern of increasing uniqueness or divergence among these models as we moved from the national sample (Chapter 3) to the graduates of the models' respective training programs (Chapter 4). A comparison of these two samples *within* each family therapy model (Chapter 5) further reinforced the importance of the supervision and training process as a significant vehicle through which family therapists are either attracted toward and/or socialized within a particular and substantively distinct orientation to the practice of family therapy. It appears, therefore, that intensive training and supervision within each family therapy model enables family therapists to identify more accurately the uniqueness of that particular model, as well as to incorporate this uniqueness into their own clinical practice.

In the present chapter, therefore, we will focus our attention on issues pertaining to the training and supervision of family therapists, by addressing two interrelated perspectives. First, we will attempt to develop a "conceptual map" of the goals of the supervisory process and in so doing suggest how these same three models of family therapy tend to align with respect to these goals. Second, we will attempt to

[1]The authors wish to express their appreciation to Dwight McCall, M.A., for his assistance in the retrieval and review of the literature and in the revision of a preliminary draft; and to Jaclyn Miller, Ph.D., for her helpful comments on an earlier draft of this chapter.

move beyond this conceptual map in order to consider how the learning process unfolds and thus how these varied goals of the supervision and training process might be viewed in a more holistic framework concerned with professional growth and development.

At the outset, it should be stressed that we choose to address both perspectives because of two assumptions emerging from our research. The first is that the family therapy literature is neither comprehensive nor detailed enough to permit a systematic comparison of the three models of family therapy on their respective supervision and training goals. Similarly, the literature lacks the empirical data bases on both the processes and outcomes of each model's supervisory activities necessary to permit the same goodness-of-fit test as we were able to utilize in the preceding chapters. Hence, our attempts to develop a conceptual map of the goals of supervision and to interface this map with the three models of family therapy represents but a preliminary extrapolation from our earlier findings of divergence among these models. Clearly, more systematic empirical attention to the differences in approaches to training family therapists is urgently needed in the field. Perhaps our conceptual map may provide a reference point for such efforts.

The second assumption upon which this chapter's dual perspectives are based reflects the central theme of this book. While the identification of similarities and common themes across models of family therapy is not to be ignored, as Bateson (1979) observed, new knowledge emanates from the observation of differences. In this chapter, as has been the case in preceding chapters, we will seek to identify and acknowledge the richness provided through diversity in the training and supervision of family therapists. Our attempt to move beyond a conceptual map of the goals of supervision and toward a generic model for the learning process, therefore, is done to preserve and legitimize this very diversity within the field. In so doing we also hope to suggest how the varying approaches to the practice of family therapy and the training of family therapists might share the same vehicle, even if they choose to disembark at different sites.

As noted, the previous chapters have documented the existence of such diversity within the practice of family therapy; therefore, if we accept the views of a broad philosophical spectrum of clinicians who argue that the goals (and processes) of supervision in fact tend to mirror the goals and processes of the therapeutic enterprise (Aponte, 1982; Fleming & Benedek, 1966; Haley, 1977; Lewis, 1978), then such diversity also abounds in the far less systematically explored arena of the training and supervision of family therapists. In applying a more generic learning model to the supervisory process, therefore, we hope to avoid the premature closure so inevitable when family therapists attempt to argue in behalf of certain goals of supervision as opposed to others, just as we trust that the previous chapters' findings have cautioned against premature closure on behalf of one set of belief and/or action systems as opposed to another in the practice of family therapy.

The Stochastic Model

It is perhaps quite appropriate that we should begin this discussion of the training and supervision of family therapists by citing Bateson's (1979) explication of the stochastic model. Bateson described the stochastic process as "a sequence of events combining a random component with a selective process so that only certain outcomes of the random are allowed to endure" (p. 253). Furthermore, this process might be depicted as requiring three sequential, albeit overlapping, stages: exploration, selection, and consolidation. As Byng-Hall and Whiffen (1982) note,

> Initially the elements in this collection are not related to each other in any specific way. They are brought into interaction with each other. This we call an exploratory phase. The interaction between them will result, however, in those which articulate with each other combining, while others drop out. Selection has occurred. At some point the interacting elements will have formed a system, that is a new whole with unique properties dependent on the relationships between the elements. This we will call a consolidation phase. [pp. 5–6]

The task of the exploration phase, therefore, is a system change function. For the professional development of the family therapist, the challenge is one of creating more flexible and permeable "boundaries" around one's existing belief and/or action systems, so that new information is sought out and one's receptivity to a "flood of new ideas" (Byng-Hall & Whiffen, 1982, p. 6) is maximized. The task of the selection phase, on the other hand, is a system survival function. New ideas must be sifted out on the basis of their potential rewards and effectiveness in solving existing problems and/or impasses. Obviously selection can occur only where the tension created by the exploration phase's "flood of new ideas" is strong enough, while it is made necessary to prevent this tension from becoming immobilizing for the learner/practitioner. Finally, the task of the consolidation phase is a system-maintenance function. This provides the learner/practitioner with a resting place from which new ideas, once selected, can be integrated and a newly defined boundary around one's belief and action systems can be formed.

To the casual eye these three phases may appear to represent a linear model. However, when we stretch this sequence into a circular loop, we can appreciate quickly the paradoxical nature of the consolidation phase of learning. On the one hand it is a necessary stage in solidifying the incorporation and integration of newly acquired knowledge, skills, and/or values. Such integration is essential in providing the grounding for a family therapist's evolving sense of professional identity and competence. Yet, at the same time, consolidation may promote solidification and resistance to change. Hence, the task of training and supervision becomes one of how to jar the family therapist into moving toward the next stage of consolidation and toward renewed exploration and selection, without undermining the previously established consolidation phase and without threatening this evolving identity and sense of professional competence. Each new consolidation stage, therefore, represents a particular learning task or goal that is significant for the professional's developing competency. Indeed, the same task may reappear at several different consolidation stages, over time.

Furthermore, when we adopt this view of the professional development process, it becomes obvious that different clinicians "begin" at different places in terms of the consolidation stages or tasks they have mastered previously and therefore the new learning yet to be explored. What appears to distinguish approaches to supervision and training within the family therapy enterprise is the differential emphasis placed upon varied learning tasks and upon the methods of supervision utilized in achieving the consolidation of such tasks. Inevitably, however, all learners must be jarred, and Minuchin and Fishman's (1981) description of therapy as the art of "joining while challenging" seems highly appropriate for the supervisory enterprise as well, for it too must challenge the learner to new exploration while at the same time supporting those growth stages previously consolidated. Or, as Whitaker (1982) observed, training and supervision in family therapy must keep the trainee at the point of dynamic balance (and tension!) between growth and homeostasis.

Goals of Supervision:
"Consolidation" Tasks

A review of the literature on supervision and training suggests several issues around which the tasks or goals of the supervisory process tend to polarize. While certainly not exhaustive, Haley's (1977) discussion of some of these polarities, or what he described as Z to A orientations to training, provides an important introduction. One such issue pertains to the degree of responsibility assigned to the trainer for achieving change, not simply in the trainee but also in the family system. A second issue or polarity focuses attention on the relative importance placed upon the supervisory process as a model for personal growth as opposed to skill or technique development. A third polarity relates to the teaching/learning medium and addresses the relative benefits and deficits of utilizing self-report as contrasted with live observation within the supervision and training process. Perhaps the most crucial issue, however (which also relates to the personal growth versus technique polarity just noted), focuses on the importance of insight or self-awareness in promoting the clinician's professional development. This debate, in turn, interfaces with the importance assigned to theory (and therefore clinical assessment) as guiding or being guided by (used to explain) intervention. Indeed, some of these same polarities also are evidenced in the previous chapters' findings pertaining to the practice arena, such as the stronger value placed upon the Insight and Professional Growth assumption factors by the communications and Bowenian models of family therapy, the distinctly stronger value placed upon the Therapist as Theoretician assumption factor by the Bowenian model's adherents, and the distinctly stronger value placed upon the Therapist as Director assumption factor by the structural/ strategic model's adherents.

When one steps back from these debates, however, and asks what the essential core of the therapeutic enterprise is, most would agree with Lewis (1978) that it is the therapeutic relationship itself. No particular polarity, therefore, provides a generic strategy for the supervisory process. Just as no particular theoretical framework, belief system, or interventive technique alone promotes the goals of therapy, so too can the same be said for the goals of supervision and training. Rather, all of these factors (and others) represent, in their composite patterning and packaging (albeit unique for each clinician), the elusive but essential holism described as the therapeutic relationship. No one part of this package is sufficient, as all parts must interrelate in a harmonious, systematic way. Yet, as Minuchin (1981) so poignantly describes, this whole in turn also must become something more than merely the sum of its parts.

In Figure 6–1 we attempt to portray the significant consolidation tasks or goals of supervision that contribute to this holism called the therapeutic relationship. Not surprisingly, the model portrayed in Figure 6–1 aligns itself with L'Abate and Frey's (1981) ERA typology of

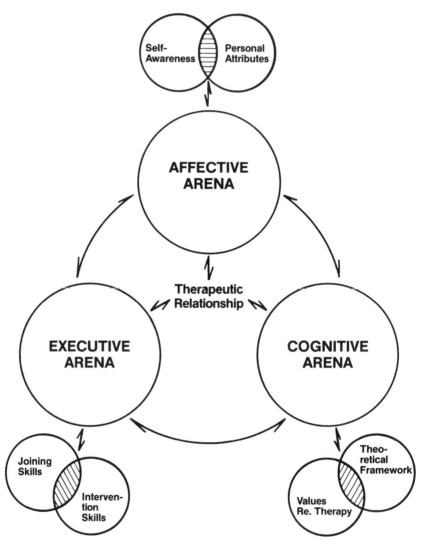

FIGURE 6-1 Consolidation Tasks or Goals of Supervision.

orientations to the practice of family therapy, portrayed in Table 2–12, by recognizing the affective, cognitive, and behavioral or executive tasks that must be mastered as the clinician moves from one consolidation stage to the next within the supervisory process. Indeed, if in fact the supervisory process mirrors the clinical process, it would not be difficult to infer that the previously described alliances between the practice of the three models of family therapy and each of these three arenas also equally applies to the way each model supervises or trains family therapists. But, perhaps more important, Linehan (1980) best summarized it by suggesting that while one can distinguish models of supervision and training by the relative emphasis each places on action versus emotions versus cognitions as targets of change for the trainee, the critical task of supervision is to help in developing accurate clinical assessments (cognition), in implementing treatment strategies related to these assessments (actions), and in understanding how one's own values and beliefs impact upon both of these processes (affect).

Affective Arena

In the affective arena, we identify two interrelated domains as goals of the supervision and training process. The first stresses the importance of the personal growth of the family therapist through increased insight and self-awareness (Ard, 1973; Berman, 1979; Ekstein & Wallerstein, 1972). The debate within this domain centers around the role of personal therapy in the professional development of the family therapist. Some would argue that the task of personal growth through increased insight and self-awareness can be confined to the supervisory process and identified and addressed essentially within the context of therapeutic impasses between the trainee and his/her clients (Aponte, 1982; Kadushin, 1976; Napier & Whitaker, 1973). Others argue that personal therapy is a critical prerequisite to or adjunct of the supervisory process (Duhl & Duhl, 1979; Fleming & Benedek, 1964). Still others focus this directive more clearly toward the importance of family-of-origin work (Framo, 1979; LaPerriere, 1979; Whitaker, 1981), which enables therapists to become more aware of their own personal scripts or "hookers" that may diminish their effectiveness in working with families. From our previously reported findings on the practice of family therapy, probably the Therapist as Theoretician, Therapist as Risk-taker, Professional Growth, and Insight assumption factors all provide the strongest interface with this domain; with the first strongly valuing the importance of history and the impact of one's family of origin on present functioning, and the latter three stressing the importance of self-awareness and insight in accurately interpreting the meaning of others' communication patterns, as well as the impact of one's own patterns on others.

The second domain within the affective arena pertains to personality attributes. In Chapters 3, 4, and 5 we provided some contour to this domain by identifying those personality attributes uniquely descriptive of each family therapy model, as well as those attributes strongly descriptive as well as nondescriptive across all three family therapy models. For example, we found that Trusting, Self-assured, and Emotional Stability were attributes highly descriptive of all three models, while their polar opposites (Suspicious, Apprehensive, and Affected by Feelings) were least descriptive across these three models. We also found that each model varied in the degree to which its adherents displayed unique personality profiles. For example, the communications model's adherents scored highest on Venturesome, Forthright, and Tenderminded, while the Bowenian model's adherents scored highest on Self-assured, Self-sufficient, and Controlled. Interestingly, the structural/strategic model's adherents displayed no uniquely divergent personality attributes.

While still an area urgently in need of more intensive empirical exploration, a consistent clustering of critical personality attributes does emerge from the available literature addressing the goals of training and supervision in family therapy. Perhaps the essence of these attributes is captured by Whitaker (1982) in his discussion of the need to expand the creative potential and spontaneity of the trainee, and of the potential danger that adherence to a particular set of techniques creates by diminishing the family therapist's capacity to be flexible and responsive to new ideas or approaches. Others describe this consolidation task as one of promoting eternal learners (Duhl & Duhl, 1979; Gurk, 1979; Hess, 1980), while still others describe this domain in terms of the flexibility to risk and to self-disclose (Haley, 1977), which is anchored by a sense of confidence about one's self as a clinician (Kniskern & Gurman, 1979).

Cognitive Arena

With regard to the cognitive arena, the consolidation tasks again fall into two domains. The first, theoretical framework, can be captured best by discussions emphasizing the need for developing a cognitive map for understanding and assessing human systems (Everett, 1979; Ferber, 1969; Kadushin, 1976). This map requires a sound base in family systems theory and communication patternings (Berman, 1979; Cleghorn, 1973), in the developmental stages of families (Duhl & Duhl, 1979), in interactional structures (Aponte & Van Deusen, 1981), in individual pathology and normal development (Everett, 1979; Ferber, 1969), as well as in the observational skills prerequisite for making such assessments (Constantine, 1976). Furthermore, our previously reported findings on the practice of family therapy suggest that the

Systemic View assumption factor may interface with the argument on behalf of developing a cognitive map, that the Family Role Structure assumption factor may provide directives for (part of) the contour of this map, and that the Problem Solving assumption factor may argue on behalf of the observational and assessment skills attendant to this task.

It should be underscored, however, that at issue is *not* which theoretical frameworks are selected, but rather that the exploration, selection, and consolidation processes directed toward this particular cognitive task of developing a theoretical framework be placed on the agenda for the training and supervision of family therapists. Indeed, oftentimes we make the mistake of "flooding" the learner with too many theoretical frameworks, thereby resulting in frustration or negativism rather than functional selection activities.

Similarly, *when* the choice of theoretical orientations is made is not at issue within the supervisory process. To be sure, both questions are important ones that influence the debate concerning how to enhance the professional development of clinicians most effectively. Lacking empirically based directives for guiding such decisions, however, perhaps we can say fairly that the different models of family therapy stress different theoretical frameworks for assessing family systems and indeed place differential weight upon the importance of theory as a prerequisite grounding for the learning of interventive techniques.

The second consolidation task within the cognitive arena pertains to therapeutic belief systems. In Chapters 3, 4, and 5 we provided some contour to this domain in assessing areas of convergence and divergence among the three models of family therapy on two sets of assumption factors or belief systems. Further elaboration on this domain in the context of the goals of supervision and training of family therapists is offered by Heath (1983) and Wessler (1980), who emphasize the importance of the clinician developing an ideology about how problems occur, why they are maintained, and how they can be changed. This clearly relates to how one defines normal or healthy family systems (Lewis, 1978; Lewis, Beavers, Gossett, & Phillips, 1976), as well as to one's general perspective about cause and effect when viewing the locus of dysfunctioning (Napier & Whitaker, 1973). As Minuchin and Minuchin (1983) say, it is a question of whether or not one assumes innocence or guilt when attempting to observe and assess family systems. Finally, it should be stressed that this second consolidation task within the cognitive arena pertains to one's value system regarding the *therapeutic process* and is different from the *personal insight* sought within the self-awareness domain of the affective arena.

Executive Arena

When we move to the executive arena, once again the consolidation tasks fall into two broad domains. The first, interventive techniques, entails a wide repertoire of change strategies. In Chapters 3, 4, and 5 we provided a broader lens for viewing this domain in our comparison of the three models of family therapy on two sets of style factors. In these analyses we found a broad continuum of therapeutic interventions, from Composer and Detoxifier at one end, to Agitator and Energizer on the other. More specificity around the range of available intervention techniques is abundantly available, however, within the family therapy literature (Eshelman & Liddle, 1979; Kiesler, Sheridan, Winter, & Kolevzon, 1981; Minuchin & Fishman, 1981; Pinsoff, 1979, 1980; Tomm & Wright, 1979). Again, at issue is neither *which* techniques are to be taught, nor *when* they are introduced most effectively within the supervisory and training process, nor *how* they are best learned. Rather, it is simply to acknowledge that within this executive arena lies some of the consolidation tasks essential for the professional development of the clinician.

The second domain in the executive arena is what might be described broadly as joining skills (Minuchin & Fishman, 1981) or the core conditions (Hart, 1982; Kniskern & Gurman, 1979; Lewis, 1978; Tomm & Wright, 1979) of empathy, genuineness, and positive regard that most clinicians agree are the essential building blocks of the therapeutic relationship. Affirmation of the importance of this domain also can be drawn from Chapters 3, 4, and 5, where the Attender intervention style factor consistently was rated as the most descriptive in-session behavior by the respondents across all three family therapy models.

Before concluding our discussion of the goals of supervision, a final comment appears warranted. While the debate abounds within the family therapy field regarding the relative importance of the consolidation tasks represented within each of the six domains portrayed in Figure 6–1, these choices are made more complicated when decisions are to be made *within* each domain as to which direction of personal self-discovery the affective arena might take, or which theoretical framework(s) the cognitive arena might prescribe, or, finally, which interventive techniques are to assume the focus of attention within the executive arena. It is in the context of these varied choices, confronting both the trainer and the trainee, that the family therapy profession reflects its diversity and complexity. Lacking empirical evidence by which to direct these exploration and selection choices, perhaps it is more important to emphasize the fact that particular intervention techniques (whichever might be selected) tend to be grounded in particular theoretical frameworks about human systems and, indeed, in particular beliefs about the therapeutic change process.

Amid this complexity, therefore, what may become more significant are two more generic principles. First, that theoretical framework and interventive techniques should be isometric to be learned effectively (Green & Kolevzon, 1982), whichever ones are selected and in whichever order they are taught. Second, the attempt to integrate new information derived from any of these six domains must have reverberative consequences on the remaining five domains. Hence, as the consolidation of tasks is achieved in one arena, it should catalyze renewed exploration and selection (and ultimately consolidation) in the other two arenas as well.

When viewed in this context, finally, the issue of whether a trainer begins with theory and works deductively to refine techniques, or begins with techniques and inductively builds theory, may be a far less significant one. Perhaps it is analogous to arguing that Detoxifying interventive techniques should be learned before learning Energizing techniques. Ultimately, whichever consolidation task is chosen, all three arenas must change interactively in seeking a new level of integration. Where the trainer begins may be an important consideration for each model of family therapy, but this decision also must vary for each learner, out of respect for the consolidation tasks she/he thus far has mastered along the path toward professional development.

While at a general level these principles may sound comforting, at the more pragmatic level they present difficulties for the beginning family therapist's attempts to define the direction(s) of his/her own exploration process. They also present difficulties for the more advanced clinician, who is attempting to achieve a certain degree of "eclecticism" by integrating a broader range of consolidation tasks across all six domains.

In the case of the beginner, while we are respectful of the random component ascribed by Bateson to the stochastic process, we do believe that one's exploration can be guided by exposure to the varying orientations to practice within the family therapy field and by testing the "goodness of fit" between each of these orientations and one's own perspectives. It is in this context that we have developed and tested an instrument (Kolevzon & Green, 1983), based upon the data set presented in Chapter 4, with which to guide the beginning family therapist's exploration process (see Appendix B of this book).

With regard to the advanced clinician, however, the path is far less clear. Liddle (1982), for example, has warned of the dangers of eclecticism. We, in turn, would caution that one danger of prolonged exploration (and delayed selection) may be a false sense of competency—knowing a little about a lot. Another caution might be the very limits of eclecticism, wherein the attempt to consolidate new tasks in fact may undermine previously mastered ones. In these contexts it is important to reaffirm our previous findings that, in fact, diversity and divergence do exist within the family therapy profession. This diversity should not be minimized by the equally important task of seeking commonalities or areas of convergence within the profession, nor should it be replaced by a more closed-system orientation that insists upon a preference among "competing" theoretical frameworks and/or interventive techniques.

Indeed, in the end it is conceivable that therapeutic effectiveness may be more dependent upon the isometry between one's affective, cognitive, and executive arenas of professional functioning than it is upon the specific theoretical framework or interventive techniques selected from these respective domains. If so, the critical supervision and training issue becomes one of building logically and sequentially upon previously mastered consolidation tasks. The challenge of training, therefore, is one of timing and sequencing, not excluding and including. This, in turn, requires that the supervisor choose those teaching modalities and processes that will help to jar the clinician from his/her particular resting place or plateau at the last consolidation stage, toward new exploration, selection, and consolidation for the other five remaining domains, as well. It is to these learning modalities and processes within the supervision and training of family therapists that we now turn.

Methods of Supervision:
Exploration and Selection Tasks

Although not as clearly defined as such, when we explore the literature we find similar polarities in the debate over the most effective supervision and training modalities by which to guide the family therapist's professional development. This debate actually exists on two levels. The first pertains to the relative efficacy of specific teaching/learning modalities. The second pertains to the relative merit of a training process that moves inductively from techniques, as contrasted with one moving deductively from theory.

With regard to the first level, while it can be said safely that the family therapy movement provided significant impetus for the use of live supervision (Berger & Dammann, 1982; Birchler, 1975; Haley, 1977; Montalvo, 1973), a review of the literature on training programs shows a wide diversity in the teaching/learning modalities utilized. Perhaps a somewhat quieter, but nonetheless significant, impetus is found in the profession's advocacy of the group supervision model as a seminar for augmenting the cognitive arena (Berg, 1978; LaPerriere, 1979), as a mechanism for promoting personal and interpersonal self-awareness within the affective arena (Coppersmith, 1980; Duhl & Duhl, 1979), as well as a medium for observation and role playing/simulation that will develop and refine interventive skills within the executive arena (Aponte, 1982; Everett, 1979; Ferber & Mendelsohn, 1969; Hart, 1982). A third impetus provided by some trainers in the family therapy movement has been evidenced by the use of cotherapists (Tucker, Hart, & Liddle, 1976; Whitaker, 1982). Others have augmented this approach by advocating the use of team teaching within the group supervision process (Ferber & Mendelsohn, 1969). Indeed, as a general statement, it might be argued that a central theme in the contribution of family therapy to the supervision and training process has been one of making its teaching/learning activities more public and directly observable. For, as Whitaker (1982) observed, ongoing personal and professional growth is a continual battle against the privacy and isolation inherent in the clinical enterprise.

While the diversity of teaching/learning modalities is indeed vast, an inspection of the descriptive profiles of the actual training programs (see, for example, *Journal of Marriage and Family Therapy,* July 1979) presents an interesting phenomenon. We immediately discover the very same movement toward eclecticism in the teaching/learning modalities used within the practice of supervision as we frequently find within the practice of family therapy. It is not simply that different learning modalities are utilized to promote different supervisory goals, but rather that, as the diversity of supervisory goals expands, inevitably so too does the diversity of modalities utilized to achieve each of these goals. Hence, the problem of selecting appropriate teaching/ learning activities becomes far more complicated.

Similarly, if the family therapy profession lacks adequate empirical grounding for determining which therapeutic techniques are effective in achieving what kinds of changes in family systems, the same concern can be voiced even more strongly with regard to the supervision and training of family therapists. It appears inevitable that, within both the practice and the supervision of family therapists, this push toward eclecticism in belief and action systems will move far more quickly than empirical efforts to disentangle systematically this ever-increasing web of complexity. Yet, while it is difficult enough to deal with this push toward eclecticism within the practice arena, this same push within the family therapy training and supervision arena creates an even more multidimensional problem for the trainer. The complexity of the goals and techniques of practice quickly becomes interwoven intimately with the complexity of the goals and techniques of the supervisory process.

Consequently, the best way to address this debate concerning varied teaching/learning modalities within the supervision and training process, again, is to avoid the closed-system, "either/or" perspective of selecting from "competing" technologies. Instead we must reframe these issues at a second and substantively different level of abstraction. At such a level, the most critical thread running through these discussions of training modalities focuses upon whether the trainee learns best by moving inductively and experientially from technique to theoretical framework (Constantine, 1976; Ferber & Mendelsohn, 1969; Gershenson & Cohen, 1978; Haley, 1977), or by moving deductively from theory and assessment toward techniques (Boyd, 1978; Everett, 1979; Kadushin, 1976; Lewis, 1978). In these discussions, where one begins tends to become the focal point of emphasis in the training and supervision process, while where one ends tends to assume a less significant role (indeed, one that is altogether ignored by some). Or, from another perspective, beginning inductively tends to place greatest emphasis upon the consolidation tasks within the executive arena, whereas beginning deductively tends to direct greatest attention toward the cognitive arena.

We would argue, however, that a more functional way to view the supervision and training process is to regard *both* inductive and deductive processes as necessary components of the entire learning experience. Furthermore, we would suggest that they evolve in a sequential patterning that can be captured within the context of the stochastic model's movement from exploration to selection to consolidation stages. While we might propose as an aspiration that professional development and learning is a lifelong task, it is clear that each learner arrives at a particular supervisory or training experience with a degree of grounding in certain competencies or previously mastered consolidation tasks. The complexity and challenge of the supervision and training process obviously is that different learners may converge at the same training experience with different interests and abilities regarding the directions they might want to move within the context of that particular training experience.

Despite these differences, the first crucial challenge of the learning process is to jar the trainee toward new exploration and away from the homeostasis reinforced by his/her previously mastered competencies. To achieve this, a structured, experiential, indeed agitating experience is preferred (Byng-Hall, Carteret, & Whiffen, 1982; Kirk & Kolevzon, 1978; Loganbill, Hardy, & Delworth, 1982). While this should be viewed as an inductive and experiential process, it is *not* synonomous with developing either the interventive techniques or joining skills domains within the executive arena. Movement toward the consolidation tasks of self-awareness and personal insight in the affective arena also can be jarred through inductive experiences such as Kagan's "interpersonal process recall" method (1969, 1975), where self-assessment and analysis based upon viewing one's own clinical practice tapes is utilized. Similarly, movement toward expanding one's theoretical frameworks and belief systems about practice in the cognitive arena also can be jarred inductively, by having trainees first review and assess tapes of family interactions, such as those structured by the Beavers-Timberlawn evaluation format (Lewis et al., 1976).

The point bears reemphasis. Each trainer's decision to jar the learner toward new consolidation tasks in *either* the affective, cognitive, or executive arena is a complex one. It is guided by where the learner begins (i.e., the consolidation tasks previously mastered), by the trainer's own value system regarding what constitutes effectiveness as a clinician (i.e., which consolidation tasks are most important), as well as by his/her model of the proper sequencing for learning these consolidation tasks. We do propose, however, that this jarring process (irrespective of the consolidation task that is selected) can best be catalyzed through structured, experiential, inductive learning experiences.

Once this jarring has occurred and the learner moves into the exploration phase that begins a new learning cycle (or spiral), deductive learning experiences become critical. Here the delicate balance is one of providing the trainee with a broadened panorama of the domain, without overwhelming him/her. Once again, deductive learning is not necessarily synonymous with developing either the theoretical framework or belief system domains within the cognitive arena. Exposure to a range of interventive techniques or joining skills within the executive arena, or exposure to the role of self-awareness and personal insight within the affective arena, also can be expanded during this exploration stage, through lectures, reading, observation, and/or group seminar discussion formats.

As noted, the goal of broadening the trainee's exposure to clinical practice in any of the six domains must be tempered by the danger of creating such a comprehensive and complex panorama that it will immobilize the learner. At some critical point in this exploration phase, therefore, the learner's "surge" toward eclecticism may leave him/her vulnerable to feelings of frustration and helplessness. At this critical point it becomes necessary for the supervisor to push the trainee into the selection phase, forcing a narrowing of the field through trying out and experimenting with specific techniques, theoretical frameworks, and the like, as appropriate to the particular domain under exploration. This selection process clearly becomes a "doing" phase; therefore, structured, experiential, and inductive teaching/learning experiences once again become critical.

While the lines between each phase of this learning process can never be drawn or delineated clearly, Figure 6–2 provides a visual representation of the flow within the learning process as it relates to the stochastic model.

Ultimately, the challenge for the trainee occurs at two critical points. The first is the "jarring" experience, which pushes her/him from homeostasis and consolidation toward growth through renewed exploration. The second is the "overwhelmed" experience which pushes her/him from continued exploration toward selection. The subsequent consolidation of these newly selected tasks, and hopefully the higher plateau of clinical competency derived from this consolidation process, emerges, in turn, through continued practice, evaluation, and feedback.

For the trainer, on the other hand, the challenge is far more complicated and demanding. Despite possessing a broader view or image of the whole and of the complexity of the clinical enterprise, she/he continually must shield this wider lens so as to help the learner to move from exploration to selection (and ultimately consolidation). Knowing that some (indeed many) pieces of the puzzle inevitably must remain behind as the learner selects specific tasks to consolidate is perhaps the most frustrating of all positions for the trainer. It demands infinite patience and an almost blind faith in the change process; faith that the trainee's successful completion of the last stochastic cycle intrinsically will jar her/him into new cycles of exploration, selection, and consolidation. It is through actualization of this faith that the lifetime learner emerges.

Toward Eclecticism

Not coincidentally, in its own way the preceding section of this chapter represents its own jarring experience regarding that ultimate tier of family therapy, a level of eclecticism in clinical practice wherein the

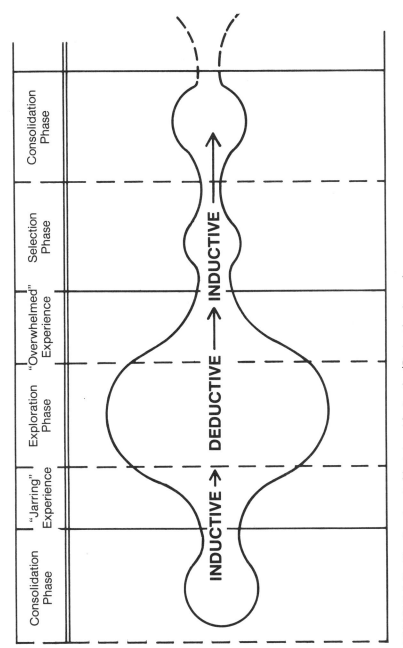

FIGURE 6-2 The Stochastic Model and Inductive/Deductive Learning.

clinician is knowledgeable about the full range of belief and action systems within the profession and purposefully selects those thought to be appropriate and effective in each particular case situation. As has been the format and theme throughout this book, we will explore this phenomenon of eclecticism from our own data base, but, before doing so, two cautions are in order.

First, it should be underscored that our study's sampling and instrumentation plan inherently limited the parameters of our operationalization of eclecticism to the three models of family therapy under investigation. Obviously other family therapy models therefore have been excluded, and thus so too has the boundary of our definition of eclecticism. Second, the lack of adequate empirical information on the effectiveness of various family therapy models (Gurman & Kniskern, 1978, 1981; Wells, 1978) compounds the issue of eclecticism. For, if we are not clear about what techniques achieve what outcomes for whom, how can we "purposefully" combine or multiply the uniqueness of each model in the training of an eclectic clinician? Presented from another vantage point, if we attempt to combine approaches to family therapy and fail, we will not know if our failure resulted from selecting the wrong approach for a particular case until we *first* know that, in fact, we can implement that approach with competence.

Therefore, we may find it useful to distinguish between two levels of eclecticism. The first level represents a largely random, trial-and-error approach that in all probability undermines that crucial holism or integration between the three arenas discussed previously. The second level, on the other hand, represents an ideal that clinicians might strive for, with patience, but also with the full knowledge that it may (or should) never be fully achieved.

Indeed, as we argued previously, it is probable that, as one attempts to widen or expand one's repertoire of interventive techniques, there may come a point when certain techniques are strategically incompatible with or philosophically antithetical to other techniques. The use of paradoxical interventive techniques may be one such example. Similarly, we would argue that certain theoretical frameworks or belief systems may present a view of human behavior and interpersonal interaction that is inconsistent with other frames of reference. The importance of power and hierarchical structure within the family system may be one such example. At what point, therefore, does the expanding nature of the clinician's belief and action systems begin to undermine the clinician's movement toward isometry between the affective, cognitive, and executive arenas? Unfortunately, this is a question we can raise only as we move forward to explore the phenomenon of eclecticism.

Methodology

In studying eclecticism, we will turn to our known-group data set, largely because of the more significant impact that intensive training has exhibited in influencing the practice of family therapists. Combining the respondents from all three family therapy models (N = 157), we divided this sample into two groups: eclectics and noneclectics. The eclectic group (N = 30) was comprised of respondents whose scores on the revised Theoretical Orientation Scale were at or above the mean for *all three* of the family therapy models' subscales (despite the fact that they received intensive training in only one model). The noneclectic group (N = 70), on the other hand, was composed of respondents who scored at the mean or above, exclusively, on only one model of family therapy. By way of introduction, it might be of interest to note that 20 percent of the communications model's original known-group sample were assigned to the eclectic group, as compared to 27.5 percent from the Bowenian model's known group and only 5.7 percent from the structural/strategic model's known group ($p < .0002$).

Comparing the Groups:
Belief Systems (Assumption Factors)

In looking at the five assumption factors created from the national sample (Chapter 3) and the seven assumption factors created from the known-group sample (Chapter 4), we find that the eclectic group scored significantly higher than the noneclectic group on seven of these 12 factors. The most striking pattern of significant differences appeared to cluster within both domains of the affective arena, with eclectics scoring significantly higher on the Insight and Professional Growth assumption factors; and within the values domain of the cognitive arena, with eclectics scoring significantly higher on the Therapist as Risk-taker and Therapist as Facilitator assumption factors. Surprisingly, however, no significant differences emerged when comparing the two groups on their valuing of the Therapist as Theoretician and Systemic View assumption factors.

Overall, the most highly valued assumption factors for the eclectic group were Family Role Structure, A-traditionalism, and Therapist as Facilitator; while the least valued assumption factors were Family Responsibility, Family Participation, and Therapist as Director. Because of the relative underrepresentation of the structural/strategic model's adherents in the eclectic group, the eclectics' strong valuing of the first two assumption factors lends added significance to the role these factors may play as dimensions of eclectic practice. The pattern of least valued assumption factors poses a potential dilemma for the clinician, however. How does one minimize family responsibility and participation while at the same time also minimizing therapist as director?

Comparing the Groups:
Action Systems (Style Factors)

When comparing the eclectic and noneclectic groups on the six style factors created from the national sample and the six from the known-group sample, even fewer significant differences emerged. Indeed, only on the Modeler assumption factor derived from each sample did the eclectic group score significantly higher. Overall, the most descriptive style factor for the eclectic group was the Attender, reflecting the importance assigned to the joining skills domain of the executive arena; while the least descriptive style factors were the more active roles of Agitator and Energizer, perhaps reflecting the under-representation of structural/strategic model adherents in this eclectic group.

Comparing the Groups:
Personality Attributes (16PF)

When comparing the eclectic and noneclectic groups on the 16 personality factors, once again, few significant differences emerged. Indeed, the eclectic group scored significantly higher only on two of the 16 factors: Self-assured and Tenderminded.

Comparing the Groups:
Background Data/Practice Activities

Finally, perhaps the most startling finding is the fact that this same pattern of convergence strongly predominates when comparing the eclectic and noneclectic groups' prior experiences and current practice activities. More specifically, when looking at prior professional experiences, no significant differences emerged when comparing these groups on their age or sex, or on their years of direct practice experience in working with families, individuals, or groups. Interestingly, in looking at nonclinical activities, however, the eclectic group had significantly more years of experience in supervision, staff development, and teaching. Since the eclectic group's respondents were not significantly older and also displayed no significant differences in their years of clinical practice experience, one might infer from these collective findings that the eclectic group's respondents tended to invest their relatively similar time span of professional functioning in a more diverse range of both clinical and nonclinical activities. Finally, with regard to the respondents' current practice, once again no significant differences were found when comparing the two groups on their percentage of current cases devoted to either family, individual, or group therapy; on the length of their caseloads; on the proportion of cases in which varying units of treatment were seen or preferred; and, finally, on the proportion of cases in which varying presenting problems were identified or preferred.

Comparing the Groups: Summary

Overall, we are struck by the lack of consistent divergence or significant differences between the eclectic and noneclectic groups. This pattern was most evident when the respondents' actual practice was viewed, either from the perspective of their in-session behaviors (style factors), their prior clinical experiences, or their current practice activities and preferences. Collectively these findings should offer some support for the need to take pause about this phenomenon of eclecticism and to wonder whether it may be more one of form and promise (or pretense) than one of substance.

Indeed, the present findings might be interpreted as suggesting that it is easier to add to one's repertoire of interventive techniques than it is to add to one's theoretical framework or belief system. In so doing, however, are we producing level-one or level-two eclectics? As noted previously, the push toward eclecticism is an inevitable part of the professional development of the clinician. Indeed, as this book attests, when reframed as a "segmentation" process, this push also appears to be an inevitable part of the very development or evolution of the family therapy profession itself. The ultimate test for both, clinician and profession, is therefore rooted in how patiently and effectively each selects and consolidates in response to the "overwhelmed" experience that this push inalterably creates.

References

Aponte, H. J. The person of the therapist: The cornerstone of therapy. *Family Therapy Networker*, 1982, *6*, 19–21.

Aponte, H. J., & VanDeusen, J. M. Structural family therapy. In A. S. Gurman & D. P. Kniskern (Eds.), *Handbook of family therapy*. New York: Brunner/ Mazel, 1981.

Ard, B. N. Providing clinical supervision for marriage counselors: A model for supervisor and supervisee. *The Family Coordinator*, 1973, *22*, 91–98.

Bateson, G. *Mind and nature: A necessary unity*. New York: Bantam Books, 1979.

Berg, B. Learning family therapy through simulation. *Psychotherapy: Theory, Research and Practice*, 1978, *15*, 56–60.

Berger, M. & Dammann, C. Live supervision as context, treatment and training. *Family Process*, 1982, *21*, 337–344.

Berman, E. & Dixon-Murphy, T. Training in marital and family therapy at free standing institutes. *Journal of Marital and Family Therapy*, 1979, *5*, 29–41.

Birchler, G. R. Live supervision and instant feedback in marriage and family therapy. *Journal of Marriage and Family Counseling*, 1975, *1*, 331–342.

Boyd, J. D. *Counselor supervision: Approaches, preparation, practices*. Muncie, Ind.: Accelerated Development, Inc., 1978.

Byng-Hall, J., Carteret, J., & Whiffen, R. Evolution of supervision: An overview. In Rosemary Whiffen & John Byng-Hall (Eds.), *Family therapy supervision: Recent developments in practice*. London: Academic Press, Inc., 1982.

Cleghorn, J. M. & Levin, S. Training family therapists by setting learning objectives. *American Journal of Orthopsychiatry*, 1973, *43*, 439–446.

Constantine, L. Designed experience: A multiple, goal-directed training program in family therapy. *Family Process*, 1976, *15*, 373–388.

Coppersmith, E. The family floor plan: A tool for training assessment and intervention in family therapy. *Journal of Marital and Family Therapy*, 1980, *6*, 141–145.

Duhl, F. J. & Duhl, B. C. Structured spontaneity: The thoughtful art of integrative family therapy at BFI. *Journal of Marital and Family Therapy*, 1979, *5*, 59–75.

Ekstein, R. & Wallerstein, R. S. *The teaching and learning of psychotherapy*. New York: International Universities Press, Inc., 1972.

Eshelman, M. A. & Liddle H. *The family therapist behavior inventory*. Philadelphia: Temple University, 1979.

Everett, C. A. A master's degree in marriage and family therapy. *Journal of Marital and Family Therapy*, 1979, *5*, 7–13.

Ferber, A. & Mendelsohn, M. Training for family therapy. *Family Process*, 1969, *8*, 25–32.

Fleming, J. & Benedek, T. Supervision: A method of teaching psychoanalysis. *The Psychoanalytic Quarterly*, 1964, *33*, 71–96.

Fleming, J. & Benedek, T. *Psychoanalytic supervision*. New York: Grune and Stratton, 1966.

Gershenson, J. & Cohen, M. Through the looking glass: The experiences of two family therapy trainees with live supervision. *Family Process*, 1978, 17, 225–230.

Green, R. G. & Kolevzon, M. S. Three approaches to family therapy: A study of convergence and divergence. *Journal of Marital and Family Therapy*, 1982, 8, 39–50.

Gurk, M. D. & Wicas, E. Generic models of counseling supervision: Counseling/instruction dichotomy and consultation metamodel. *Personnel and Guidance Journal*, 1979, 57, 402–407.

Gurman, A. S. & Kniskern, D. P. Technolatry, methodolatry and the results of family therapy. *Family Process*, 1978, 17, 275–281.

Gurman, A. S. & Kniskern, D. P. Family therapy outcome research: Knowns and unknowns. In A. S. Gurman & D. P. Kniskern (Eds.), *Handbook of family therapy*. New York: Brunner/Mazel, 1981.

Haley, J. Problems in training family therapists. In J. Haley, *Problem solving therapy*. San Francisco: Jossey-Bass Publishers, 1977.

Hart, G. M. *The process of clinical supervision*. Baltimore: University Park Press, 1982.

Heath, A. W. & Storm, C. Answering the call: A manual for beginning supervisors. *Family Therapy Networker*, 1983, 7, 36–37.

Hess, A. K. *Psychotherapy supervision: Theory, research and practice*. New York: John Wiley & Sons, 1980.

Kadushin, A. *Supervision in social work*. New York: Columbia University Press, 1976.

Kagan, N. *Influencing human interaction*. Washington, D.C.: American Personnel and Guidance Association, 1975.

Kagan, N. & Schauble, P. Affect simulation in interpersonal process recall. *Journal of Counseling Psychology*, 1969, 16, 309–313.

Kiesler, D. J., Sheridan, M. J., Winter, J. E., & Kolevzon, M. S. *Family therapist intervention coding system*. Richmond: Family Institute of Virginia, 1981.

Kirk, S. A. & Kolevzon, M. S. Teaching research methodology from Z to A: A backward approach. *Journal of Education for Social Work*, 1978, 14, 66–72.

Kniskern, D. P. & Gurman, A. S. Research on training in marriage and family therapy: Status, issues and directions. *Journal of Marital and Family Therapy*, 1979, 5, 83–94.

Kolevzon, M. S. & Green, R. G. An experientially based inductive approach to learning about family therapy. *The American Journal of Family Therapy*, 1983, 11, 35–42.

L'Abate, L. & Frey, J. The e-r-a model: The role of feelings in family therapy reconsidered: Implications for a classification of theories of family therapy. *Journal of Marital and Family Therapy*, 1981, 7, 143–150.

LaPerriere, K. Family therapy training at the Ackerman Institute: Thoughts of form and substance. *Journal of Marital and Family Therapy*, 1979, 5, 53–58.

Lewis, J. M. *To be a therapist*. New York: Brunner/Mazel, 1978.

Lewis, J. M., Beavers, W. R., Gossett, J. T., & Phillips, V. A. *No single thread: Psychological health in family systems*. New York: Brunner/Mazel, 1976.

Liddle, H. A. On the problem of eclecticism: A call for epistemological clarification and human scale theories. *Family Process,* 1982, *21,* 343–350.

Liddle, H. A. & Halpin, R. J. Family therapy training and supervision: A comparative review. *Journal of Marriage and Family Counseling,* 1978, *4,* 77–98.

Linehan, M. Supervision of behavior therapy. In A. K. Hess (Ed.), *Psychotherapy supervision: Theory, research and practice.* New York: John Wiley & Sons, 1980.

Loganbill, C., Hardy, E., & Delworth, V. Supervision: A conceptual model. *The Counseling Psychologist,* 1982, *10,* 3–42.

Minuchin, S. & Fishman, H. C. *Family therapy techniques.* Cambridge, Mass: Harvard University Press, 1981.

Minuchin, S. & Minuchin, P. Normal families revisited. Presentation at The Healthy Family Conference, Philadelphia, May, 1983.

Montalvo, B. Aspects of live supervision. *Family Process,* 1973, *12,* 343–359.

Napier, A. Y., & Whitaker, C. A. Problems of the beginning family therapist. *Seminars in Psychiatry,* 1973, *5,* 229–242.

Pinsoff, W. M. The family therapist behavior scale (FTBS): Development and evaluation of a coding system. *Family Process,* 1979, *18,* 151 161.

Pinsoff, W. M. *The family therapist coding system (FTCS) coding manual.* Chicago: Northwestern University Medical School, 1980.

Tomm, K. M. & Wright, L. M. Training in family therapy: Perceptual, conceptual, and executive skills. *Family Process,* 1979, *18,* 227–250.

Tucker, B., Hart, G., & Liddle, H. Supervision in family therapy: A developmental perspective. *Journal of Marriage and Family Counseling,* 1976, *2,* 269–276.

Wells, R. A. & Dezen, A. E. The results of family therapy revisited: The non-behavioral methods. *Family Process,* 1978, *17,* 251–274.

Wessler, R. & Ellis, A. Supervision in Rational-Emotive Therapy. In A. K. Hess (Ed.), *Psychotherapy supervision: Theory, research and practice.* New York: John Wiley & Sons, 1980.

Whitaker, C. A. Training and growth of the therapist. In J. R. Neill & D. P. Kniskern (Eds.), *From psyche to system: The evolving therapy of Carl Whitaker.* New York: The Guilford Press, 1982.

7

The Dilemmas of Growth

In Chapters 1 and 2 we profiled family therapy's past by tracing its evolution through the diversification process endemic to all professions. In Chapters 3, 4, and 5 we assessed family therapy's present by exploring areas of convergence and divergence in the current practice activities and belief systems of adherents to three of the most prominent models of family therapy. Our overriding concern, however, the *raison d'être* of this book, is the *future* of family therapy and a concern for and curiosity about the evolving nature and shape of family practice(s) to come. While Chapter 6 provided just such a transition by exploring the professional development of the family therapist, it is toward this future that we direct our attention in the present chapter.

Like many of the theorists, practitioners, and commentators of the family therapy movement previously described, we too regard the idea and implementation of family therapy as representing much more than an additional treatment modality in the mental health enterprise's arsenal. We share the view of many that family therapy may be an expression of a fundamental shift in the thinking that guides this enterprise. Indeed, as Haley suggests, it also may represent, through its accentuation of the social determinants of human behavior, one of the major historical discoveries humans have made about themselves and their world (Haley, 1980).

Consequently, we also share the hopes of many in the field that the growth of the family therapy movement and the knowledge and skill bases that provide its foundation will continue with vigor. However, we share the concerns of our colleagues regarding the *nature* of the growth of this movement. Indeed, as we argued in Chapter 1, a major dilemma confronting the evolving profession of family therapy is one of maintaining its efforts to expand, diversify, and verify its knowledge and skill bases while at the same time identifying and preserving the bridges of common beliefs and techniques that unify the profession and guide the growth and development of its members. To address this dilemma, we suggested the need for a clearer inventory of both the shared and divergent characteristics of family therapy practice, and we created one such empirically based inventory of the similarities and differences among three of the most historically prominent models of family therapy. In so doing, we have confirmed numerous assertions regarding areas of convergence and divergence among the three models. We also have raised questions about other previously existing areas of (presumed) knowledge. Reciprocally, we hope that both our confirmations and questions will stimulate and direct future verification efforts.

On another level, we also are pushed to an analysis of the future of family therapy by a series of larger and perhaps more fundamental questions. Three of these questions are particularly pivotal to the growth of this interdisciplinary profession and are discussed here. These questions, each representing a "dilemma of growth" for the family therapy field as a whole, are concerned less with the nature of the diversity in the field and more with the management of that diversity—perhaps the major challenge facing the profession in the 1980s and beyond.

Who Speaks for Family Therapy?

The findings from the previous chapters provide ample evidence of the diversity existing within the interdisciplinary profession of family therapy, of the uniqueness of varying approaches to the practice of this profession, and finally of the contribution made by each family therapy model in transmitting this diversity to subsequent generations of clinicians. At the same time, we must be mindful of the strong unifying forces within the profession. One significant example is the effort on behalf of licensing family therapists and accrediting family therapy curricula in graduate-level programs. While the American Association for Marriage and Family Therapy presently has assumed the pre-eminent role of guiding both of these efforts, the fact still remains that many clinicians who are providing marital and family therapy are doing so in private and public agencies as well as in private practice settings without having received either licensing from AAMFT or graduate degrees from programs accredited by this association.

Indeed, the truly interdisciplinary nature of the family therapy profession, paradoxically, actually may help to increase the number of such clinicians. As Bloch and Weiss (1981) noted, for example, disciplines such as clinical and counseling psychology and social work, each with their own licensing and accrediting standards and processes, continue to expand their offerings of family systems theory and family therapy clinical internships within their own graduate curricula. It is not altogether certain, for example, that graduates of accredited master's- or doctoral-degree programs within such allied fields, having been exposed to family therapy in their course work and possibly practice, and having received licenses within their own discipline, will feel the urgency of also meeting the additional standards established through AAMFT licensing.

How important these ancillary routes become as alternative paths for preparing clinicians to practice family therapy will have important ramifications for the profession's efforts to achieve quality control and accountability through the standards it requires for accrediting programs and licensing family therapists. In all probability, free-standing family therapy training institutes, such as those studied in our known-group survey, will continue to carry a significant responsibility for refining and deepening the knowledge, value, and skill bases of those who choose these alternative pathways. Yet this, in turn, confronts the clinician with the complexities inherent in selecting and participating in the best training programs for strengthening her/his particular clinical bases. At the same time it also confronts the family therapy profession with the difficulties and conflicts inherent in determining which training centers meet the desired standards and which do not. In the end, might not the exponential growth of the number of clinicians providing family therapy also make it impossible to establish acceptable guideposts along all of these varied pathways?

Not unlike the social work profession at the turn of this century, formal family therapy training has its roots in the agency-based practicum model. However, it now sees the university-based educational model assuming a more significant role in the setting of standards for the preparation and licensing of its practitioners. Presently, within the social work profession the free-standing agency-based training center has become virtually extinct. Its educational function has been directed largely toward in-service staff development and, in some instances, field practicum settings for students seeking BSW, MSW, and doctoral degrees. Indeed, even the role of continuing education in the social work profession currently is housed largely within academic institutions.

It will be important, therefore, for the family therapy profession to recognize that, while certain advantages accrue from such an evolutionary process, it is not without potential liabilities. Presently the free-standing family therapy training centers provide important opportunities for ongoing supervision and training of AAMFT members. They also provide professional development opportunities ranging from educational enrichment to intensive training for many other clinicians, perhaps some of whom ultimately also will seek AAMFT membership. All of these professionals, however, are engaged in the clinical enterprise and are attempting to enhance their effectiveness, and many are benefited by the important educational resources provided by these training facilities.

Perhaps more important, these training facilities historically have provided an essential catalytic axis around which the uniqueness of each particular model of family therapy has been defined, refined, evaluated, and ultimately disseminated to the consuming public. In its legitimate push toward developing and enforcing accreditation and licensing standards, therefore, it is essential that the profession continue to maintain a significant role for such training facilities and for the preeminent practitioners/educators/researchers they likely will continue to attract. The danger of any move toward standardization is that the richness provided through diversity tends to dissolve under the pressure for developing a "common core" or "unifying theme." While achieving this unification process confounds the clinician, educator, and family therapy researcher alike, it also potentially undermines the profession's own vitality by promoting sameness and by discouraging differentness and experimentation.

How Many Voices Can Be Heard?

When we speak of the vitality provided by a diversity of orientations to the practice of family therapy, we also must acknowledge the pitfalls of such diversity as well. How different are, in fact, these models of family in their actual practice? More important, are the differences between these models better predictors of therapeutic effectiveness than are the similarities? Segmentation within an evolving profession and attempts by each segment to develop and disseminate the uniqueness of its particular approach to practice are both unavoidable parallel forces within the family therapy profession. The challenge is not one of preventing these forces but rather one of managing them most effectively. It is a challenge, in turn, that confronts both the individual clinician as well as the profession as a whole.

For the individual family therapist, the dilemma is not unlike the "overwhelmed" experience resulting from a "flood of new ideas" described in Chapter 6. Even the most cursory review of recent editions of *The Family Therapy Networker,* for example, leaves one exhausted by the abundance of family therapy workshops from which to choose. It also stimulates our curiosity as to whether the clinician's choice is based upon professional development needs, geographic and/or financial accessibility, the desire to "encounter" a prominent "pioneer" of the field, or the "appeal" of the location where the workshop will be held.

Excited by the new horizons opened by this burgeoning field of practice, the family therapist's initial response simply may be one of "trying everything," in the hopes that an infusion of the broadest spectrum of ideas will provide catalytic directives for new selection and consolidation tasks. Just as likely, however, a clear directive will not be evident. Indeed, the potential complexity and even conflictual nature of these new ideas may frustrate or dampen this initial excitement. Under such circumstances, the aspiring family therapist ultimately may be confronted with the equally unenviable choices of either a more-or-less asystematic "level-one eclecticism" or a "don't bother me with the facts" solution. Either approach merely strengthens the morphostatic potentials of any previously mastered consolidation task; hence, the lifetime learner becomes transformed into a lifetime critic and cynic. Change and diversity become viewed with boredom, seen as reinventions of one's own wheel (or as others' dysfunctional square ones) rather than as opportunities to discover more effective ways to help families cope with the problems of living.

By some means, therefore, the family therapy profession must preserve ways of socializing its members into possessing a healthy respect for diversity and for the specialized knowledge, values, and skill bases that this diversity represents. Similarly we believe that the profession has the responsibility of communicating to its members that patience, sequence, and timing are essential ingredients when attempting to expand one's clinical repertoire. It is perhaps ironic that the profession's own segmentation process, so vital to its growth and development, may communicate the opposite message to its members, thereby endangering their own vitality. In the end, if a profession's members lose their vitality, so too does the profession.

But What Voice Do We Listen To?

Unlike the individual practitioner, however, the profession of family therapy cannot cope with the dilemmas of growth by chaotically "trying everything" or by rigidly retrenching and "trying nothing." Clearly, given the equally diverse and growing number of constituencies seeking accountability within the family therapy movement, more morphogenic choices are required.

Fortunately, as we have previously recounted, the practice of family therapy is no stranger to the scientific enterprise. Clearly, it emerged in a research context and it continues to be shepherded by the scientific method. However, science (fortunately) does not dictate the solution to such problems; it only provides direction through methodological rules and avenues by which answers may be sought.

Within the family therapy profession in the 1980s, a number of methodological directions for the management of diversity have been suggested and debated by professionals concerned with the scientific advancement of family therapy practice. Two not mutually exclusive directions, however, seem to us to be the most fundamental to those debates. The first is concerned primarily with theory. Its proponents advocate for the development of a generic theory of family therapy practice, suggesting that much of the espoused diversity in the field is more illusory than real. Indeed, grounded in the belief that many similar family theory and therapy concepts merely appear different because they are labeled and prioritized differently by proponents of different approaches to family therapy practice, a number of "integrated" models recently have been constructed, while others are apparently forthcoming.

A second methodological direction currently is being advocated with even more urgency. It focuses on the need for more adequately designed and executed outcome studies on the effectiveness of family therapy practice. Advocates for this direction, perhaps reflecting the coming of age of the field, are increasingly assigning a higher priority to designs that provide for the comparison of two or more approaches to family therapy, than to those designs that involve the comparison of family therapy with no treatment or with individual treatment. Rather than producing a single generic or integrated theory, many of the advocates of this position see the evolution of a number of situationally specific theories of family therapy, informed by repeated empirical examination, and applicable to diverse problems, situations, and client populations.

While the purpose of our study was neither to develop a generic or integrated theory of family therapy practice nor to evaluate or infer the effectiveness of the three models of family therapy we have compared, we do think that our findings give reason to pause for those concerned with the former methodological direction, while providing guidance for those who aspire to the latter. With regard to the development of a generic theory of family therapy, the nature and pervasiveness of the divergence among the three family therapy models suggest to us that, at this historical point in the evolving professionalization process, such integrative attempts run the risk of producing a model of practice that may be internally inconsistent, difficult to operationalize, and therefore therapeutically ineffective.

Clearly, our data have suggested that the differences among the three models are more of "substance" than they are of emphasis. In many cases, the intensively trained practitioners, in particular, hold polar and perhaps mutually exclusive belief systems about family theory and therapy, while their action systems often are characterized by behaviorally antithetical dimensions of interventive style. Consequently, attempts to merge these three models may result in theoretically complex and inclusive practice blueprints that may be too cumbersome and abstract for the practitioner to interpret and operationalize with any fluidity. Furthermore, as we noted previously, it may very well be that, within a prescribed range of beliefs and behaviors, therapeutic effectiveness is more a function of the congruency between what a therapist believes and what a therapist does, rather than a function of the particular belief or action system employed in the therapeutic process. If this is the case, the construction of a generic theory from the three models investigated in this study also risks the elimination of a potential source of therapeutic effectiveness.

Obviously, and with regard to the second methodological direction, our study does not add directly to the cumulative knowledge about the relative efficacy of the different models of family therapy. However, the lack of clarity with which treatment models have been described in the past has posed problems with the interpretation of comparative studies of individual as well as family therapy. Unfortunately, and again reminiscent of individual psychotherapy, knowledge acquired from process research, which concerns itself with the observation, specification, and understanding of the nature of therapeutic processes, has been in most cases either absent or at best minimally present. It is our hope, therefore, that our identification of the convergent and divergent parameters of each model, as well as the similarities and differences among the individuals oriented to each, will shed light on the results of previous outcome studies and aid in the design of those comparative studies yet to come, as well as stimulate additional contributions to the family therapy process and descriptive research literature.

Ultimately, the confusion with regard to the interpretation of findings that has resulted from the historical imbalance between process and outcome research has been costly to the understanding and consequently the credibility of individually oriented treatment methods. Unfortunately, the even greater paucity of family therapy process research, coupled with the growing push for more comparative outcome studies, may have a similar impact on the family field. Indeed, it is foreseeable that the disillusionment with which practitioners and consumers greeted both the inconsistent and the negative findings that accompanied the growth of an outcome literature for the individual therapy methods may in fact be replicated within the family therapy field.

On the other hand, and illustrative of what we see as one of the numerous partnerships necessary for managing the diversity in the family therapy field, the choice for future research must not be made between either process or outcome research. Rather, these two forms of investigation must complement, mutually reinforce, and provide corrective feedback to one another. Indeed, just as there may be a sequence to how a clinician learns and to how a profession unfolds, evolves, and segments, so too might there be a sequence to how a profession and its practitioners are studied.

References

Bloch, D. A., & Weiss, H. H. Training facilities in marital and family therapy. *Family Process*, 1981, *20*, 133–146.

Haley, J. *Leaving home.* New York: McGraw-Hill, 1980.

Appendix A

Items from the Revised Theoretical Orientations Scale

Family Therapy Model	Author	Publication	Concepts
Communications	Satir	*Conjoint Family Therapy*	"Personal freedoms" "Communication" "Congruence"
Bowenian	Bowen	"Toward a differentiation of self in one's family"	"Family projection process" "Triangles" "Differentiation"
Structural/ Strategic	Haley	*Problem Solving Therapy*	"Boundaries" "Alignments" "Joining"
	Minuchin	*Families and Family Therapy*	

Appendix B

The Family Therapist's Belief and Action Systems Scales (FTBASS)

This appendix includes the *revised* (1983) Family Therapist's Assumption Scale and Family Therapist's In-session Style Inventory. In addition, scoring keys for each are provided, to enable individuals to complete these instruments and group their responses according to the assumption and style factors created from the responses of the graduates of the three training programs discussed in Chapter 4. Having done so, one then can compare one's *own* belief and action system preferences with the profiles provided for these three models of family therapy, thereby identifying areas of "fit" or agreement with each. All scale revisions and scoring keys are based upon the factor analyses described in Chapter 4. Finally, it should be noted that the original questionnaire included these two instruments (before revision), plus the 16PF, the Theoretical Orientation Scale, and a Background Data section. Readers interested in the original questionnaire may contact Michael S. Kolevzon, School of Social Work, Virginia Commonwealth University, Richmond, Virginia 23284.

Family Therapist's Assumption Scale (revised 1983)

The following statements reflect *assumptions* about family therapy that some therapists hold. There is by no means universal agreement on these assumptions, and similarly no right or wrong answer. Please use the scale below to circle the number that most accurately indicates the extent to which you agree or disagree with each of these statements.

SCALE

1. strongly disagree   4. slightly agree
2. moderately disagree   5. moderately agree
3. slightly disagree   6. strongly agree

1. A central focus of family therapy is one of clarifying the roles and relationships within and between the varying subsystems of the family.   1 2 3 4 5 6

2. Much of the process of family therapy focuses on the ways in which family members send messages, the ways in which family members receive and interpret these messages, and the difficulties arising from a lack of understanding between sender and receiver.   1 2 3 4 5 6

3. Change in family members' feelings about themselves and each other can be effected by showing them alternative patterns of behaving.   1 2 3 4 5 6

4. An extensive family history should precede family treatment.   1 2 3 4 5 6

5. The therapist cannot avoid becoming an interacting member of the family system.   1 2 3 4 5 6

6. Family therapy should be more concerned with the present than with the past.   1 2 3 4 5 6

7. A therapist should respect and support the differences in authority inherent in the role structure of the family.   1 2 3 4 5 6

SCALE

1. strongly disagree   4. slightly agree
2. moderately disagree   5. moderately agree
3. slightly disagree   6. strongly agree

8. A family therapist should avoid emotional interchanges among family members and focus on rational processes.   1 2 3 4 5 6

9. Family therapy is not the appropriate model of intervention in all case situations.   1 2 3 4 5 6

10. Behind every child's problem is a marital problem.   1 2 3 4 5 6

11. A therapist should take responsibility for directing the course of family therapy.   1 2 3 4 5 6

12. Change in a family system can be effected when working with only one member of the family.   1 2 3 4 5 6

13. To be effective, the family therapist should provide alternative interpretations for family members' behaviors.   1 2 3 4 5 6

14. A family therapist should share his/her perceptions of verbal and nonverbal behavior with family members in order to enable better understanding of the impact of their behavior.   1 2 3 4 5 6

15. Appropriate self-disclosure by the therapist is a vital part of the conduct of family therapy.   1 2 3 4 5 6

16. Change in family member behaviors can be effected by helping each member to deal with his/her feelings about self and about the other family members.   1 2 3 4 5 6

17. By re-enacting or "mirroring" family members' patterns of relating, a family therapist can enable the family members to recognize their own behaviors and the impact of their behaviors on each other.   1 2 3 4 5 6

SCALE

1. strongly disagree   4. slightly agree
2. moderately disagree   5. moderately agree
3. slightly disagree   6. strongly agree

18. Involving young children in family therapy hinders the conduct of the therapeutic process.   1 2 3 4 5 6

19. To become effective as a family therapist, the use of video tape or the presence of the supervisor in the actual therapy sessions is essential.   1 2 3 4 5 6

20. Changes in family members' ways of relating can be effected by their learning new ways of relating to the family therapist.   1 2 3 4 5 6

21. If a family member shares information with the family therapist, it should be shared with all members of the family.   1 2 3 4 5 6

22. A family member can best effect change in his/her patterns of relating to present family members by effecting change in the patterns of relating to his/her family of origin.   1 2 3 4 5 6

23. The use of a cotherapist enhances the effectiveness of the conduct of family therapy.   1 2 3 4 5 6

24. The family therapist ultimately is responsible for whether or not change occurs within a family.   1 2 3 4 5 6

25. Regardless of the nature of the presenting problem, all members of the family should be involved on a continuing basis in family therapy.   1 2 3 4 5 6

26. Responsibility for the content and conduct of the family therapy session should be assumed by the family members.   1 2 3 4 5 6

Family Therapist's Assumption Scale Scoring Key (revised 1983)

Factor 1

Please add together your circled responses to the following Assumptions Item Numbers:

Items: 4, 6 (*reverse,* by subtracting your score from 7), 8, 9 (*reverse*), 10, 12, and 22.

Total score _____

(divide by 7)   Item mean _____

Factor 2

Please add together your circled responses to the following Assumptions Item Numbers:

Items: 13, 14, 15, 20, and 23.

Total score _____

(divide by 5)   Item mean _____

Factor 3

Please add together your circled responses to the following Assumptions Item Numbers:

Items: 2, 3, 16, and 17.

Total score _____

(divide by 4)   Item mean _____

Factor 4

Please add together your circled responses to the following Assumptions Item Numbers:

Items: 5, 19, and 24.

Total score _____

(divide by 3)   Item mean _____

Factor 5

Please add together your circled responses to the following Assumptions Item Numbers:

Items: 18 (*reverse,* by subtracting your score from 7), 21, and 25.

Total score _____

(divide by 3)   Item mean _____

Factor 6

Please add together your circled responses to the following Assumptions Item Numbers:

Items: 11 (*reverse,* by subtracting your score from 7) and 26.

Total score _____

(divide by 2)   Item mean _____

Factor 7

Please add together your circled responses to the following Assumptions Item Numbers:

Items: 1 and 7.

Total score _____

(divide by 2)   Item mean _____

Now enter your *item means* below:

Factor 1: _____ (Therapist as Theoretician)
Factor 2: _____ (Therapist as Risk-taker)
Factor 3: _____ (Therapist as Facilitator)
Factor 4: _____ (Therapist as Director)
Factor 5: _____ (Family Participation)
Factor 6: _____ (Family Responsibility)
Factor 7: _____ (Family Role Structure)

Note: Higher item mean indicates factor is *more* descriptive of your belief system.

Family Therapist's In-session Style Inventory (revised 1983)

Let's assume that as therapists we all vary our behavior to meet the needs of different types of families and different phases in the therapy process. Yet, in spite of these variations, we all have some sense of the *general style* that describes our work with families. Please try to convey a picture of your general style by circling the number that most accurately reflects the degree to which each of the following items describes your general style in the therapy process.

		Not at all *Descriptive*				*Extremely* *Descriptive*	
1.	Teaching	1	2	3	4	5	6
2.	Directing	1	2	3	4	5	6
3.	Supporting	1	2	3	4	5	6
4.	Reflecting	1	2	3	4	5	6
5.	Provoking	1	2	3	4	5	6
6.	Listening	1	2	3	4	5	6
7.	Reacting	1	2	3	4	5	6
8.	Organizing	1	2	3	4	5	6
9.	Arbitrating	1	2	3	4	5	6
10.	Observing	1	2	3	4	5	6
11.	Questioning	1	2	3	4	5	6
12.	Modeling	1	2	3	4	5	6
13.	Agitating	1	2	3	4	5	6
14.	Interpreting	1	2	3	4	5	6
15.	Confronting	1	2	3	4	5	6
16.	Participating	1	2	3	4	5	6
17.	Reality Testing	1	2	3	4	5	6
18.	Persisting	1	2	3	4	5	6
19.	Analyzing	1	2	3	4	5	6
20.	Neutralizing	1	2	3	4	5	6
21.	Planning	1	2	3	4	5	6
22.	Comic	1	2	3	4	5	6
23.	Casual	1	2	3	4	5	6
24.	Consistent	1	2	3	4	5	6
25.	Expert	1	2	3	4	5	6

Family Therapist's In-session Style Inventory Scoring Key (revised 1983)

Factor 1

Please add together your circled responses to the following Style Item Numbers:

Items: 2, 5, 7, 9, 13, 15, 18, and 25.

Total score _____
(divide by 8)   Item mean _____

Factor 2

Please add together your circled responses to the following Style Item Numbers:

Items: 6, 10, 11, and 24.

Total score _____
(divide by 4)   Item mean _____

Factor 3

Please add together your circled responses to the following Style Item Numbers:

Items: 3, 12, 16, and 17.

Total score _____
(divide by 4)   Item mean _____

Factor 4

Please add together your circled responses to the following Style Item Numbers:

Items: 8, 20, and 21.

Total score _____
(divide by 3)   Item mean _____

Factor 5

Please add together your circled responses to the following Style Item Numbers:

Items: 4, 14, and 19.

Total score _____

(divide by 3)   Item mean _____

Factor 6

Please add together your circled responses to the following Style Item Numbers:

Items: 1, 22, and 23.

Total score _____

(divide by 3)   Item mean _____

Now enter your *item means* below:

Factor 1: _____ (Energizer)
Factor 2: _____ (Attender)
Factor 3: _____ (Modeler)
Factor 4: _____ (Planner)
Factor 5: _____ (Analyzer)
Factor 6: _____ (Composer)

Note: Higher item mean indicates factor is *more* descriptive of your in-session Style.

Index

Index